The
History
of
BODMIN JAIL

Compiled, edited and arranged from Contemporary Sources

by

Bill Johnson

Published by

Bodmin Town Museum,
Mount Folly, Bodmin, Cornwall, PL31 2HQ

The Title

The institution for criminals in Bodmin has been known as Bodmin Gaol; the County Gaol, Cornwall; H M Prison at Bodmin; and Bodmin Jail. The latter spelling has been chosen as the book title for two reasons, firstly, the Act of Parliament, published in 1778, was entitled *'An Act for building an additional Jail...'* and, secondly, in recent times, the *Jail* spelling has been used for the night club and later the tourist attraction and restaurant. Throughout the book the alternate spelling, *gaol,* has been used as this is the most common spelling in published documents.

About the Author

Bill Johnson, Ph.D., is a graduate with degrees in chemistry who has spent his working life in the pharmaceutical industry, researching auto-immune diseases and potential new treatments. He has published many research papers, articles, and patents and given many lectures in Europe and the United States, on the subject of enzyme inhibitors. Now retired, he has lived in Bodmin for eight years and does voluntary work for Bodmin Town Museum, involving photography, art-work for exhibits and publishing.

This book is the result of many queries from both locals and visitors regarding the buildings and life in Bodmin Jail. It is also by way of a challenge issued many years ago by a friend and colleague, the late Dr Antonin Kroehn of Prague, who claimed that the education of British scientists was too narrow and that scientists were not able to talk or write about non-scientific issues. Well Toni, if you are watching, this is the author's attempt at a piece of social history.

Also Published by Bodmin Town Museum:

A Social History of BODMIN UNION WORKHOUSE
by Tony Philp (ISBN 0-9549913-0-3)

Published by Bodmin Town Museum, Mount Folly, Bodmin, Cornwall, PL31 2HQ.
Manuscript prepared for publication by W H & J M Johnson, the publishing team.

ISBN 0-9549913-1-1

Printed by MPG Books Ltd, Bodmin, Cornwall

Contents

Dedicated to my family,
Jan & Carole
and to the
Future of the Jail

I would like to thank the following people and organisations:

Mrs Maureen Tooze, curator of Bodmin Town Museum, for access to documents and photographs, including *'The State of Prisons'* by Howard and the Victorian Statute Books. The John Soane's Museum, London, for permission to publish the *'John Call Engraving'*. Councillor Frank Stone, Mr Peter Davies, Mr Dudley Prout, Mr Christopher Smith and Mr & Mrs Ken Allen for useful discussions and permission to publish photographs and documents. The Cornish Studies Library, Redruth, for permission to use a photograph from the *'Ellis Collection'* and the Cornwall Records Office for providing copies of broadsheets, Quarter Sessions records and many other documents. Ms. Suzanne Rix, Social Policy section, British Library, for providing an index to Parliamentary Papers and the staff at Bodmin Library for their help in obtaining these Papers. The National Archive, Kew, and the House of Lords Records Office for providing copies of documents. The owners of Wildish's Builders for permission to photograph the buildings from their premises.

A book about the gaol would not be possible without the free access to the buildings provided to me by the owners of the gaol, Simon, Helen and David Wheten and their family and staff. I am grateful to them for their interest and discussion.

W H Johnson
January, 2006.

4

CHAPTER 1

Introduction

Bodmin Gaol, built in 1779, was the first modern prison built in England and was designed according to the reformist ideas of John Howard (1726-1790).

Howard,[1] a philanthropist, embarked for Lisbon in November 1755, *'for the purpose of assisting to alleviate the suffering caused by the great earthquake, that had recently laid the city in ruins'*. However, the ship was captured by a French privateer, and the crew and passengers were taken into Brest, where they were treated with extreme cruelty. The sufferings which he underwent and witnessed during his captivity appear to have made a deep impression on him. When he was released he brought the case of the prisoners of war to the notice of the *English Commissioners of sick and wounded seamen* and induced them to take measures for an exchange of prisoners.

Later, when Howard became sheriff of Bedford, he was already aware of the existence of abuses in the management of criminals and, as soon as he started the duties of his office, he commenced an inquiry into the horrible corruptions of the English prison system. On examining the three prisons in Bedford, he found that they were not only miserably deficient in decent accommodation, in cleanliness, air, food, and water, but that the gaoler and his subordinates had no salary, and were entirely dependent on the fees they could wring from the wretched prisoners, who were, after their acquittal by the court, detained in the gaol, in some cases for years, until they paid the fees of gaol delivery. In order to put an end to these gross abuses, Mr Howard proposed that a salary should be given to the gaoler in lieu of these fees; but the magistrates were startled at such an innovation, and refused to adopt it without a precedent.

In 1773, Howard started the first of several tours of public gaols in Great Britain and Ireland, all of which he found in a state disgraceful to a civilized country. He ultimately extended his investigation to the prisons and houses of correction in twelve foreign countries. Details of his journeys and the distance travelled later appeared in one of his memorandum books:[2]

AN ACCOUNT OF THE NUMBER OF MILES TRAVELLED ON THE REFORM OF PRISONS.	
JOURNEYS	**MILES**
In Great Britain and Ireland, 1773-6	10,318
First Foreign Journey, 1775	1,400
Second Ditto, 1776	1,700
Third Ditto, 1778	4,636
In Great Britain and Ireland, 1779	6,490
Fourth Foreign Journey, 1781	4,465
In Great Britain and Ireland, 1782	8,165
Fifth Foreign Journey, 1783	3,304
To Ireland	715
To Worcester	238
To Hertford, Chelmsford, and Warrington	602
TOTAL	42033

'To God alone be all praise! I do not regret the loss of many conveniences of life, but bless God who inclined my mind to such a scheme.'

Howard, who had called attention to the miserable state of the prisons, many of which he had visited, appeared as a witness before a House of Commons committee. This led to two prison reform bills being passed by Parliament in 1774. The first declared that all prisoners against whom no bill of indictment had been found by the grand jury, or who should be discharged by proclamation for want of prosecution, should be immediately set at large in open court, without any payment of any fee or sum of money to the sheriff or gaoler in respect of such discharge; and abolishing all such fees for the future, it directed the payment, in lieu of them, of a sum not exceeding 13s. 4d. out of public funds for every prisoner discharged.

The other bill was concerned with health and sanitation in the prisons. It required the Justices to see that all prisons within their respective jurisdictions, be scraped and whitewashed once a year at least - that the rooms be regularly washed and ventilated, that infirmaries be provided for the sick, and proper care be taken of them - to order clothes for them when needed - whenever possible to prevent their being kept in underground dungeons - and, generally, to take such measures as shall tend to restore and preserve their health.

When the acts passed into law, Howard immediately took energetic measures for carrying out the reforms, including having copies of the acts printed and sent to every prison in the land. However, the justices and gaolers tended to ignore them.

In 1777, Howard published the results of his investigations in 'The State of Prisons in England and Wales with Preliminary Observations, and an Account of some Foreign Prisons.'[3] This volume contains, in addition to detailed descriptions and remarks on all the gaols in the country, a section on proposed improvements in the structure and management of prisons and a generic plan for building a county gaol:

State of the Gaols in Cornwall (before 1776).[3]

COUNTY GAOL AT LAUNCESTON for felons

Gaoler: John Mules, Deputy, under Coryndon Carpenter Esq. Constable of the Castle. Salary, lately augmented by the County from £8 to £12 p.a.

Prisoners: Allowance, Felons, a three-penny loaf each in two days; white or brown at their option (weight in Dec. 1775, white bread 1 lb 10 oz. and brown 2 lb 2oz.)

Number of Felons: 19th Feb.1774 11; 13th Sep.1774 8; 23rd Dec.1775 6.

Chaplain: Rev. Mr. Lethbridge. Duty: Tuesday and Friday. Salary, lately reduced from £50 to £30.

Surgeon: Mr. Bennet. Salary, £15.

Remarks: This gaol, though built in a large yard belonging to the old ruinous Castle, is very small; house and court measuring only fifty two feet by forty four; and the house not covering half that ground. The Prison is a room or passage twenty three feet and a half by seven and a half, with only one window two feet by one and a half:—and three Dungeons or Cages on the side opposite the window: these are about six and half feet deep; one nine feet long; one about eight; one not five: this last for women. They are all very offensive. No chimney: no drains: no water: damp earth floors: no **Infirmary**. The yard not secure; and Prisoners seldom permitted to go out to it. Indeed the whole Prison is out of repair, and yet the Gaoler lives distant. I once found the Prisoners chained two or three together. Their provision is put down to them through a hole in the floor of the room above (used as a Chapel); and those who serve them there, often catch the fatal fever. At my first visit I found the Keeper, his Assistant, and all the Prisoners but one, sick of it: and heard that a few years before, many Prisoners had died of it; and the Keeper and his wife in one night.

I learned that a woman who was discharged just before my first visit (by the Grand Jury making a collection for her Fees) had been confined three years by the Ecclesiastical Court; and had three children in the gaol. There is no Table of Fees.

The King, of his Royal Bounty, has offered TWO THOUSAND POUNDS towards a new Gaol; but nothing is done by the County.

I WAS edified by the serious behaviour of the Chaplain at Prayers. The Prisoners respect him, and were very attentive. He has a large family: I was sorry for the late reduction of his Salary.

The Mayor sends the Prisoners weekly one shilling's worth of bread.

COUNTY BRIDEWELL AT BODMIN.

The County pays £10 a year for this Prison. It is much out of repair; and the walls round the yard not safe enough to let Prisoners use it. The night rooms are two garrets, with small sky-lights seventeen inches by twelve, close glazed. I was informed that a few years ago the Gaol-Fever was very fatal, not only in the Prison, but also in the Town. **Keepers** Salary lately raised from £20 to £28. Allowance a three-penny loaf in two days; (weight, Dec. 1775, 31 oz.) No employment. A **Surgeon** to this Bridewell; his Salary £20.

Prisoners: 14th Sep.1774   19;   22nd Dec.1775   29.

SHERIFF'S WARD AT BODMIN, The County Prison for Debtors

Keeper: Joseph Catty. Salary, £25. Fees, Debtors, £0 : 13 : 4, Besides   £0 : 4 : 1 to the Sheriff.

Prisoners: Allowance, none.

Number of Debtors: 14th Sep. 1774   19; 22nd Dec. 1775   18.

Chaplain: None. Surgeon: None.

Remarks: This prison, for which the Sheriff pays £20 a year, is out of repair. A spacious back-yard; with a stream running through it. The Keeper pays Window-tax £3 : 7 : 0, and I saw some windows were stopped up.—He said he had been Keeper above twenty years; and during the whole time had but four Prisoners who obtained from their Creditors the allowance commonly called the Groats.

FALMOUTH TOWN GAOL.

Two rooms: no court-yard: no water. 19th Dec. 1775: **Prisoners** none.

TRURO TOWN GAOL.

Built about two years ago upon a good plan. Two houses in front, for the two Sergeants at Mace who are the Keepers. Cross the yard is the Prison; which consists of four convenient rooms, two of them vaulted: no pump. 18th Dec. 1775, **Prisoners** none.

PENZANCE TOWN GAOL.

Two close rooms: no court-yard: no water. 19th Dec. 1775, **Prisoners** none.

AT PENZANCE is also A PRISON for the Hundred and Liberties of PENWITH,

The Property of Lord Arundel. Two rooms in the Keeper's stable-yard; but distant from his house, and quite out of sight and hearing. The room for men is full eleven feet square, and six high: window eighteen inches square: no chimney. Earth floor; very damp. The door had not been opened for four weeks when I went in; and then the Keeper began shoveling away the dirt.—There was only one Debtor, who seemed to have been robust, but was grown pale by ten weeks close confinement, with little food, which he had from a brother, who is poor and has a family. He said, the dampness of the Prison, with but little straw, had obliged him (he spoke with sorrow) to send for the bed on which some of his children lay. He had a wife and ten children, two of whom died since became thither, and the rest were almost starving. — He has written me a letter since, by which I learn that his distress was not mitigated, and that he had a companion, miserable as himself. — No allowance. **Keeper** no Salary: Fees 8s. 4d. every action, no Table. A year or two ago five **Prisoners**, I was informed, grew desperate by what they suffered in this wretched Prison, and broke out.   21st Dec. 1775, Prisoners 1.

LOSTWITHIEL GAOL for debtors

Is the Property of the Duke of Cornwall, Lord of the Stannaries. It was lately repaired and whitewashed. The Rules extend over the whole Borough. The Keeper told me that he lately had a Prisoner who was arrested for £6: the man had a large family, and not a bad Character; yet the Plaintiff paid him his groats for two years; and dying then, bound his Estate for the continual Payment of them: but the Insolvent Act freed the Prisoner and the Estate. **Keeper** no Salary: Fees 13s. 4d.

Debtors: 14th Sep 1774   4; 18th Dec. 1775   2.

PENRYN GAOL for debtors

ST. LEONARD'S Chapel: the Property of the Earl of Godolphin. One room thirteen feet square, six high: window about two feet by one foot four inches. **Keeper** (a woman) complained of paying Rent £4, and of the Prison window being taxed with those in her house. Dec. 19th Dec. 1775,   **Prisoners** none.

At this time Bodmin had the County Bridewell, which housed prisoners who had committed misdemeanours; it was situated at Church Stile. However there are two documents, which suggest that felons were also imprisoned in the bridewell. A lease dated 5th December, 1791, contains the following description: ' ... of all buildings and premises lying opposite to and against the South side of the church, abutting North on a street or road leading from Honey Street, otherwise Church Street, to the Priory, known as the Old Prison, together with the large walled courtledge adjoining the same premises, all of which buildings were formerly used as the Sherrif's(!) Ward Bridewell and **County Gaol**.' [4] The second document, dated 1772, is a decision of the Justices: 'As a result of the bridewell being used to hold prisoners for capital offences....... The salary of the bridewell keeper to be increased to £28 p.a.' [5]

The Sheriff's Ward at Bodmin, The County Prison for Debtors, was in Crockwell Street, at that time known as Prison Lane. The building still exists as the 'Hole-in-the-Wall' public house. The name derives from the time when relatives and friends passed food through the 'Hole-in-the-Wall' to the imprisoned debtors.

Proposed Improvements in the Structure and Management of Prisons.[3]

Situation: A County-gaol, should be built on a spot that is *airy*, and if possible near a river, or brook. I have commonly found prisons situated near a *river*, the cleanest and most healthy. They generally have not (they could not well have) subterraneous dungeons, which have been destructive to thousands: and by their nearness to running water, another evil, almost as noxious, is prevented, that is, the stench of **sewers**. I said a Gaol should be near a stream but I must annex this caution; that it be not so near as that either the house or yard shall be within the reach of floods. This circumstance was so little thought of at Appleby in Westmoreland, when their new Gaol was built, that I saw the walls marked from nine inches to three feet high by floods. IF it be not practicable to build near a stream, then an eminence should be chosen: for as the walls round a prison-yard must be so high as greatly to obstruct a free circulation of **air**; this inconvenience should be lessened by a rising round: and the prison should not be surrounded by other buildings, nor built in the middle of a town or city.

Plan: The annexed engraving represents a plan for a prison as, according to my ideas, unites the greatest advantages with regard to health, order, and security.

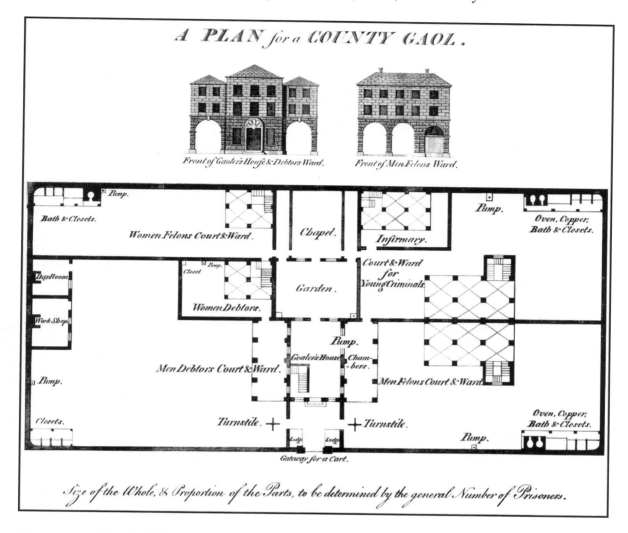

A PLAN for a COUNTY GAOL.

Front of Gaoler's House & Debtors Ward.   Front of Men Felons Ward.

Bath & Closets.

Pump.

Pump.

Oven, Copper, Bath & Closets.

Women Felons Court & Ward.   Chapel.   Infirmary.

Day Room.

Closet.   Pump.

Court & Ward for Young Criminals.

Work Shop.

Women Debtors.

Garden.

Pump.

Men Debtors Court & Ward.   Pump.   Gaoler's House.   Chambers.

Men Felons Court & Ward.

Closets.   Oven, Copper, Bath & Closets.

Turnstile.   Turnstile.

Pump.

Lodge   Lodge

Gateway for a Cart.

Size of the Whole, & Proportion of the Parts, to be determined by the general Number of Prisoners.

That part of the building which is detached from the walls, and contains the men-felons ward, may be square, or rectangular, ***raised on arcades***, that it may be more **airy**, and leave under it a dry walk in wet weather. Wards over arcades are also best for safety, for I have found that escapes have been most commonly effected by undermining cells and dungeons.

I wish to have so many **small rooms or cabins** in this ward, that each criminal may sleep alone. If it be difficult to prevent their being together in the day-time, they should by all means be separated at night. Solitude and silence are favourable to reflection; and may possibly lead them to repentance. Privacy and hours of thoughtfulness are necessary for those who must soon leave the world.

The **separation** I am pleading for, especially at night, would prevent escapes, or make them very difficult: for that is the time in which they are generally planned, and effected. Another reason for separation is, that it would free gaolers from a difficulty of which I have heard them complain: they hardly know where to keep criminals admitted to be evidence for the King. These would be murdered by their accomplices if put among them; and in more than one prison, I have seen them, for that reason, put in the women's ward.

Where there are opposite windows they should have shutters; but these should be open all day. In the men-felons ward there should be no glass; nor should the prisoners be allowed to stop the windows with straw, &c.

The women-felons should be quite **separate** from the men: and young criminals from old and hardened offenders. Each of these three classes should also have their day-room or kitchen; and their court-yard and offices all separate.

Every court should be paved for the more convenient washing it; and have a good pump or pipes laid in; both if possible: and the *Pump* and *Pipes* should be repaired as soon as they need it; otherwise the Gaols will soon be offensive and unwholesome, as I have always found them to be in such cases. A small **stream** constantly running in the yard is very desireable. In a room or shed near the pump or pipe, there should be a *Bath* to wash prisoners that come in dirty, or grow dirty afterwards. It should be filled every morning, and let off in the evening through the privies into the drains. There should also be a copper in the shed, to heat a quantity of water sufficient to warm that in the bath; for washing those that are sickly. There should likewise be an *Oven*: nothing so effectually destroys vermin in cloaths and bedding, nor purifies them so thoroughly when tainted with infection, as being a few hours in an oven moderately heated.

The *Infirmary* or sick wards should be in the most airy part of the yard, quite detached from the rest of the Gaol, and raised on arcades. In the middle of the floor of each room there should be a grate; of twelve or eighteen inches square, for a current of air; covered with a shutter or hatch at night. The same contrivance might also be convenient the other wards.

Debtors and **felons** should have wards totally **separate**: the peace, the cleanliness, the health and morals of debtors cannot be secured otherwise. The Act 22 & 23 Charles II, cap. 20, requires this separation at night; that debtors may not be disturbed by the curses and other profane language of felons. This would also remove the objection that is now made against permitting debtors to work: that is, the danger of their furnishing felons with tools for mischief, or escape.

In the debtors ward there should be a day-room or kitchen; also a large *Work-shop* for such as are willing to work. Some few Gaols have the latter and in them I have seen chair-makers, shoe-makers, &c. employed in their several trades; preserving their habit of industry; contributing to the support of their families.

Prisoners indicted for felony should not be compelled to work. But I have heard many of them wishing they might be permitted to earn something for their more comfortable support.

Women debtors should have a ward, a court, a pump &c. to themselves: and no communication should be allowed between the two sexes.

The *Ward for Men-Debtors* should also be over arcades, and placed on one side of the gaoler's house. This house should be in or near the middle of the Gaol, with windows to the felons and the debtors court-yard.

A **Chapel** is necessary in a Gaol, I have chosen for it what seems to me a proper situation. It should have a **gallery** for debtors or women; and the rest may be separated below. Bibles and prayer-books should be chained at convenient distances on each side: those who tear or otherwise damage them should be punished.

It was these ideas and designs which formed the basis of the plans for the building of the new Gaol at Bodmin.

CHAPTER 2

The Design and Building of the First Bodmin Gaol

The poor conditions at Launceston had been recognised by the Justices of the Peace in 1775, when they had written[6] to Lord North, the Lord Treasurer, *"We beg leave to represent to your Lordship how cruel the delay has already been to the unhappy wretches confined in so deplorable a place; which has at times been so bad as that the Justices of the Peace have not thought themselves justified in committing thither such persons as have been brought to them."* Lord North had offered £2,000 to the Lord Warden of the Stanneries for the building of the new gaol but no action was taken. It was nearly two years later that the Justices were informed of the offer from Lord North. They then decided that a new gaol was needed.

Launceston was ruled out as the site for the new gaol for the same reasons that the Summer Assizes had been moved to Bodmin. Launceston, 'gateway to Cornwall', was isolated from the rest of the county and the cost of transporting prisoners, paid by the parishes rather than the government, was considered a discouragement to justice. This decision confirmed Bodmin as the County Town and the site of the new gaol. *(The assizes moved to Bodmin in 1838 and the County Gaol at Launceston closed in 1829.)*

In 1778 an Act of Parliament was passed entitled, **'Act for the building of an additional Jail, and also a prison and house of correction within the County of Cornwall; and for other purposes therein mentioned'**.[7]

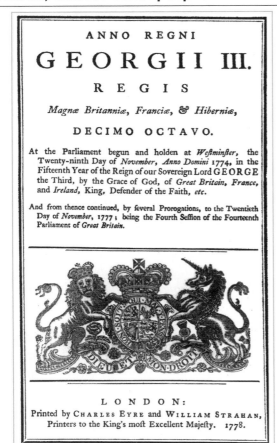

The 1778 Act of Parliament which established The County Gaol at Bodmin
Bodmin Town Museum

The Act recommended Bodmin for its clean air and pure water, early recognition that this would help in reducing disease. The Mayor and Burgesses of Bodmin had agreed to give up 'a piece or parcel of ground known by the name of Berrycombe for the site of the intended gaol'. In addition to the accommodation for criminals the new buildings were to include a new bridewell (house of correction for those found guilty of minor offences) and a new Sheriff's Ward (prison for debtors).

The gaol, which opened in 1779, was built under the supervision of John Call, J.P. *(appendix 1)*. The architect was a Mr Thomas Jones of Exeter, his foreman, James Chapple, later became governor. A post he held for nearly fifty years. The design of the prison was based on the *'Proposed Improvements in the Structure and Management of Prisons'* by Howard.

The only plans available are on a 1779 engraving (see pages 14-16),[8] sent to John Howard by John Call, which contained the following message:

> *To* John Howard *Esq. This* PLAN, ELEVATION *and* SECTION *of the* GOAL(!), Bridewell *and* Sheriff's Ward, *lately Built at* BODMIN *in the County of* CORNWALL, *is most gratefully inscribed by his very obedient humble Servant Jn. Call.*
> *As a small Token of the high Esteem, in which he holds his very indefatigable perseverance, and humane Enquiries, in behalf of his fellow Creatures unhappily deprived of Liberty during the course of many Years at the most imminent risque of his Life; and as* **a Tribute justly due to him, from whose Ideas given to the Publick the plan has been principally formed.**

The bottom section of the engraving consists of a description of the site and explains the principles behind the design of the gaol:

> *This Goal(!) is built on the side of a steep Hill facing the South on a spot rather too confined in Extent but as no more commodious Situation for Air and Water could be got, the Plan was with no small difficulty adapted to the Ground and at length so happily contrived that the Steepness of the Ground which at first appeared a great obstacle seems to be of advantage in many points, by placing the several Buildings above each other, and thereby giving each a full Sun, and fresh Air. A copious Stream of the purest fresh Water is brought in above the Goalers(!) House, and divided through every Ward to supply the Baths and other uses, and ultimately carried off through the Bog Houses. The leading principle in the disposal of the several parts of the Building is to prevent any communication of Speech or otherwise, between the different kinds of Criminals, and to keep each sex distinct by Day, and every individual separate from one another by Night. All are lodged up stairs and the Lodgings have no contact with the outer Wall so that no escape can be concerted or effected by mining. One Hundred Men and Women may be lodged in the several Wards at the same time.*

The gaol was airy and had a stream of pure water coming in at the top of the site which was piped throughout all the buildings for drinking and sanitation. There were separate areas for felons, debtors, and the bridewell. Men and women were segregated and each person had an individual cell for sleeping. All cells were built on arcades above the ground floor. This was for security and also gave a dry walk in wet weather. This arrangement was also considered more healthy because of improved circulation of air. There was an infirmary area, consisting of five rooms with a surgeon in daily attendance and as required, a chapel, dayrooms (one for each type and sex of prisoner) and a workshop.

In the Infirmary Court there were three condemned cells. In all courts there were stone troughs with a pipe and cock to supply a constant run of water. In addition there were baths, boilers to heat the water and ovens to bake the cloathes, to prevent infection and destroy vermin.

The gaoler was provided with accommodation in the main house, which contained a hall, parlour, kitchen and seven rooms for master debtors from whom he could exact fees for the privilege of living in the best part of the gaol. The turnkeys each had a chamber.

The *Call Engraving* gives a good impression of the design of the buildings but there are some problems. Firstly, the gaol was intended to house 100 inmates but from the detailed ground plan the number of cells for each type of prisoner is as follows: Common Debtors rooms, each for two people (D) 7; Chambers for Master Debtors (E) 7; Women Felons (a) 7; Women Bridewell (b) 7; Men Felons (c & e) 16; Men Bridewell (d & f) 16: Other cells included; Infirmary (B) 5 and Condemned Cells (C) 3. This only gives a total of approximately seventy inmates.

There is an inconsistency in the ground plans and the elevations. The elevations show a beautiful symmetrical building but the ground plan includes the addition of a workshop and a 'Vagrants Ward for Boys'. Both these discrepancies suggest that the engraving was a piece of art-work designed to impress Howard, and not an accurate plan of the gaol.

Howard's response to the new gaol was recorded after his visit to Bodmin in 1782:

By a spirited exertion, the gentlemen of this county have erected a monument of their humanity, and attention to health and morals of prisoners.

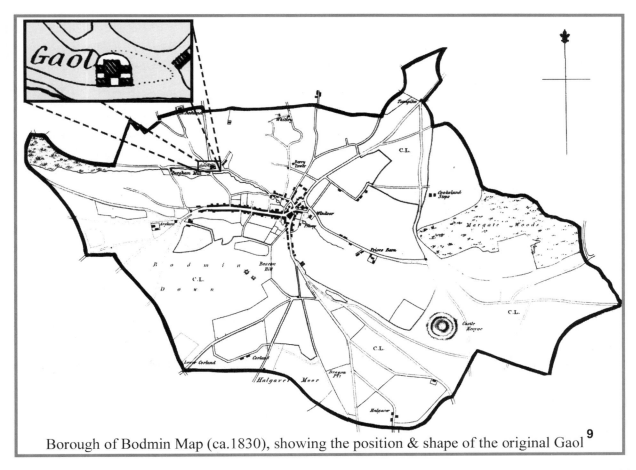

Borough of Bodmin Map (ca.1830), showing the position & shape of the original Gaol[9]

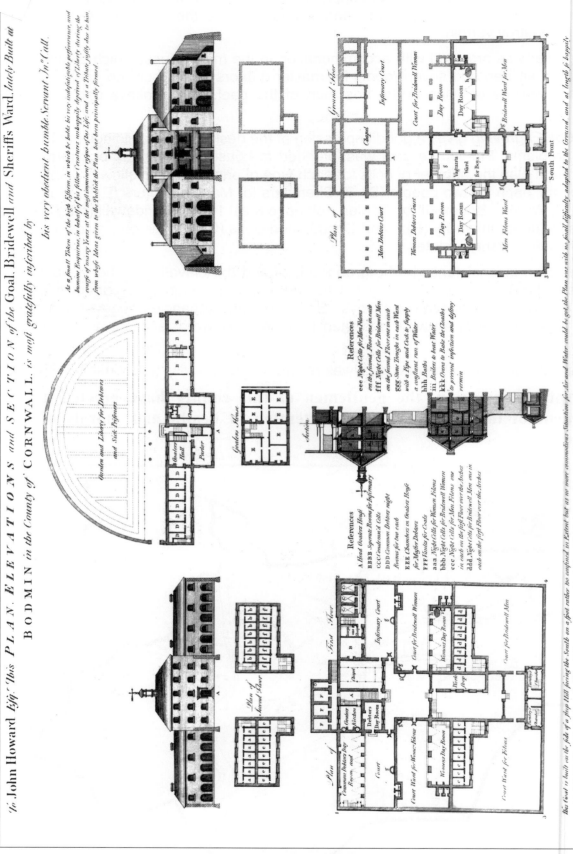

The 'John Call' Engraving.

(*Published by kind permission of The John Soane's Museum, London.*)

14

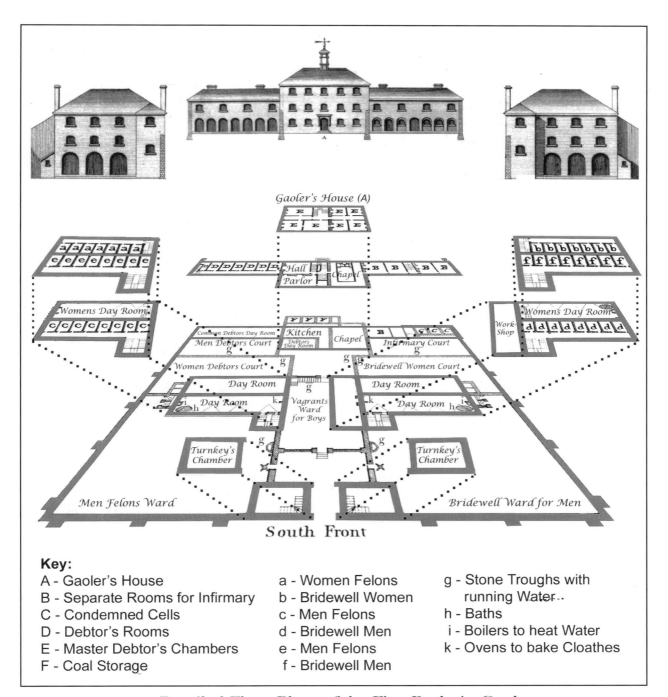

Gaoler's House (A)

Womens Day Room

Womens Day Room

Work-Shop

Common Debtors Day Room
Men Debtors Court
Kitchen
Debtors Day Room
Chapel
Infirmary Court

Women Debtors Court

Bridewell Women Court

Day Room

Day Room

Day Room

Vagrants Ward for Boys

Day Room

Turnkey's Chamber

Turnkey's Chamber

Men Felons Ward

Bridewell Ward for Men

Hall
Parlor
Chapel

South Front

Key:

A - Gaoler's House
B - Separate Rooms for Infirmary
C - Condemned Cells
D - Debtor's Rooms
E - Master Debtor's Chambers
F - Coal Storage

a - Women Felons
b - Bridewell Women
c - Men Felons
d - Bridewell Men
e - Men Felons
f - Bridewell Men

g - Stone Troughs with running Water
h - Baths
i - Boilers to heat Water
k - Ovens to bake Cloathes

Detailed Floor Plans of the First Bodmin Gaol
(Adapted from the 'John Call' Engraving)

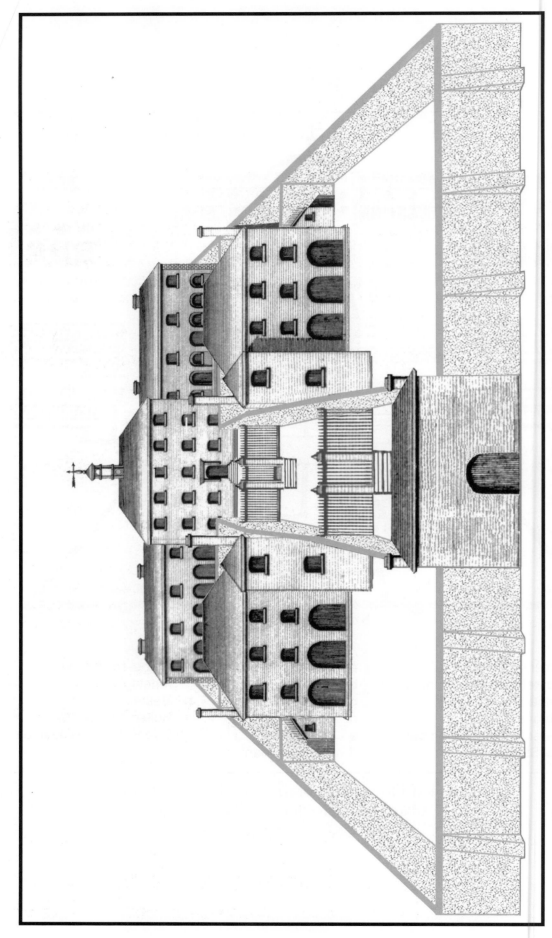

Computer Generated Image of the Gaol derived from the John Call Engraving

CHAPTER 3

The Expansion of Bodmin Gaol

The new gaol consisted of a set of elegant buildings and was considered a great advance in the care and rehabilitation of offenders. When it was built, Bodmin was one of only five gaols in the Country designed for 100 inmates. However there were problems with the function of the buildings right from the start and this led to a series of new buildings and changes. The inclusion of a workshop and a vagrants' court for boys seem to have been added to the plans before the gaol was completed. In 1780, Cornwall Quarter Sessions Records contain the following entry: ***Proposed alterations to Bodmin jail and Bridewell submitted by Mr James Chappell, keeper: stopping up 2 arcades, making a partition across the hall and adding 2 grates in the chimney there, in the women's section; stopping up 1 arcade, making a partition across the hall, making a window in each end of the passage leading to the cells, and whitewashing the cells in the men's section.*** (QS/1/4/282-291,1780).

The arcades, a key feature in the original plan, had lasted about one year. Other changes, including repairs, alterations and rebuilding, recorded in the Quarter Sessions records include:

1791 Additional buildings to the Sheriff's Ward at Bodmin completed by Joseph Beard, Architect. *(QS/1/6/168/1-182/1).*

1784 Following attempts at escape by prisoners at Bodmin Gaol, repairs to be carried out to defective walls. *(QS/1/5/1-34).*

1785 Authorisation given for the completion of repairs at Bodmin Gaol. (QS/1/5/35-63).

1805 James Chapple produced plan and estimate for alterations of turnkey's lodges at Bodmin Gaol. *(QS/1/7/317-334).*

1814 Visiting magistrates of Bodmin Gaol to consider need for erecting an additional ward at the prison for separate confinement of young persons, to procure estimates for building, and to produce their report to the court. *(QS/1/8/171-187).*

1818 Addition and alterations to Bodmin Gaol to be carried out by James Chapple, in accordance with plan and specification produced in court, not to exceed £60 in cost. *(QS/1/9/80-116).*

1820 Sum not exceeding £400 granted to improve and enlarge Bodmin Gaol, to be administered by a committee and according to plan already produced. *(QS/1/10/28-61).*

1824 Committee of magistrates appointed to consider new requirements for Bodmin Gaol and house of correction, made necessary by recent act (QS/1/10/500-531).

1825 New Sheriffs Ward to be erected adjacent to Bodmin Gaol to house thirty male debtors. *(QS/1/10/609-636).*

1827 On 1 Feb. next debtors confined in Bodmin Gaol to be removed to new building recently erected at western end of gaol, and the building to become integral part of the prison, together with such part of the gaoler's house as the sheriff shall see fit. *(QS/1/11/192-224).*

1828 Visiting magistrates of Bodmin Gaol reported that drains, ordered last year, nearly finished, greatly improved atmosphere in the gaol, and consequently in the health of the prisoners.

Since appointment of new governor many necessary repairs had been made and a contract to repair the dilapidated roof drawn up.

A new kitchen provided, where all prisoners to be served with allowance of food instead of cooking for themselves at large Fires which were kept constantly burning in their day rooms.

A laundry wash-house had been provided, where women sentenced to hard labour, would wash for the prisoners.

The apartment, previously occupied by the matron, to become the governor's office.

By building up the doorway of the Debtors' Ward and opening a way through into the gaol, the entrance to the debtors' prison would also be under the surveillance of the governor. *(QS/1/11/339-369)*.

1829 Repairs of old Bridewell progressing and separate sleeping cells being built.
Gaol yard divided into three, for separate classes of prisoners. *(QS/1/11/502)*.

1830 Governor, having reported on confined state of the chapel, too small for the increased number of prisoners, and having suggested adding an adjoining room, previously a kitchen but now vacant, for reception of female prisoners, and rearrangement of benches for the men, probable expense not to exceed £60.
Completion of all new buildings. Some repairs and alterations to old buildings remain to be done. New buildings in men's gaol now occupied. *(QS/1/11/614-657)*.

1831 Addition to turnkeys' lodges estimated at £35 but needs a further £56 as internal work had not been included.
Cast iron drop for executions ready but cannot be fixed until increased expenditure approved.
Garden wall to be raised. *(QS/1/12/60-99)*.

1832 The visiting justices hoped that the gaol expenses might have been less but noted that many repairs had been necessary to both gaol and Bridewell "built not much more than fifty years ago". *(QS/1/12/150-153)*.

1834 Visiting Justices to Bodmin Gaol empowered to buy small piece of land adjoining western end of gaol. *(QS/1/12/430-452)*.

There were further additions to the gaol in 1842 and 1847 supervised by the architect, George Wightwick of Plymouth.[10]

Some of the above reports mention sums of money but one report[11] gives an indication of the cost of the major reorganisation of the gaol. *'The justices made comparison of expenditure on gaol for four years from year ending Easter 1828 showing amounts spent on building, totalling £18,087.16s.6d.'* for comparison, the *'repairs, alterations and additions'* costs for 1843[12] and 1846,[13] were £613.6s.7d. and £167.17s.5½d.

There are three reasons for the increase in the number of buildings and the other changes in the use of buildings between 1779 and 1855.

1.   The number of committals to the gaol increased markedly during the early part of the nineteenth century. According to Redding[14], there were 105 committals in 1805, 378 in 1829 and 293 in 1839. The difference between 1805 and 1829/1839 is mainly explained by a significant increase in the population. Redding reports that the population in 1805 was 188,369. This had risen to 302,440 in 1829 and 341,269 in 1839. This was a period of industrialisation in Cornwall which led to larger towns, easier movement of people with the improved road system (and later rail system) and, in general, an increase in wealth. The increase in crime led to a higher prison population and caused

overcrowding. In 1820, several prisoners were moved to Launceston because Bodmin was full. When Launceston closed down in 1829, prisoners were transferred to Bodmin. In July, 1830, the Governor reported[15] that 'number of prisoners now *"unusually great"'*

2.   In addition to the increase in population and the closure of Launceston Gaol, the Act of Parliament in 1823, which emphasised separate confinement and the five-fold classification of prisoners also meant that the gaol needed significant change. There were now five classes of prisoners in both the gaol and the house of correction. The sexes were to be separated at all times, this meant the gaol required separate accommodation and work facilities for up to twenty different classes of prisoners. The rebuilding of the prison, from 1828 to 1833, was supervised by the new Governor, Mr Everest. The changes resulted in the number of day-rooms and courtyards increasing to 14 and the number of cells rose from 63 to 147 single and 15 double cells.[16]

3.   The 1841 census gives a total of 195 people. In addition to the 137 prisoners, it lists 13 staff members and 45 others. They included spouses (8), children (32), other relatives (2) and servants (3). This represents 30% of the inhabitants of the gaol. As the original gaol had only a few chambers for the governor and the turnkeys it would seem that additional accommodation for staff and their families must have been made available.

Plan of the Extended Gaol (1840)

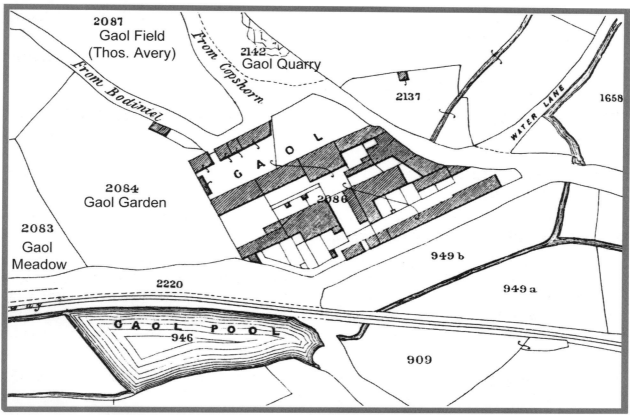

Tithe Map of 1840, showing Plan of the County Gaol at Bodmin.

The Tithe map of 1840,[17] although generally to scale, the gaol buildings and adjacent roads were hand drawn and are therefore not very accurate. The buildings on the right hand side of the site extend into the road and the end of the building is distorted in an attempt to make it fit. The walls of some of the buildings are curved and the walls are not parallel. A comparison of the Tithe map plan with the 1779 Call Engraving shows

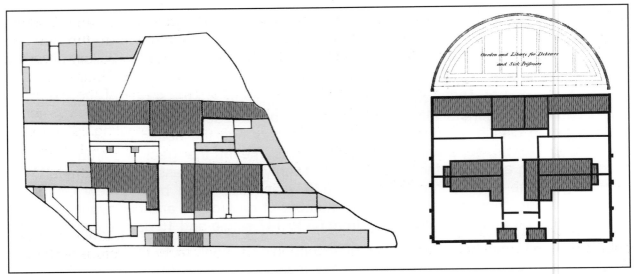

Comparison of the 1840 Tithe Plan with the 1779 Call Engraving.

that the site has been increased in area and uses parts of both the gaol garden and the garden for debtors and sick prisoners. All the original 1779 gaol buildings can be identified. The gaoler's house, with both the debtor's and the Infirmary wings is still present. The two central blocks, one with the workshop, and the two gatehouses which have been extended. Many additional buildings are present and the wards have been sub-divided. The walls in the area from the gatehouse to the Governor's house seem to be identical in both plans but the walls on the left and right of the original gaol have been removed during the extensions. One of the three sets of buildings on the left of the site must be the new debtor's prison but none of the additional buildings on the tithe map have been identified.

Water-colour entitled 'An Execution at Bodmin Gaol in 1841.' (Ref. 18)

This very colourful painting is accompanied by the following text: *"Bodmin Gaol 1841 – The fields and house behind it was called 'Copshorn', which belonged to my grandfather Thomas Pearce. (Rich? W?) P. Jago, 1865."*

The painting seems to be an accurate representation of the gaol, as judged by its position in relation to the Pearce house and the Copshorn Road. (The adjacent diagram

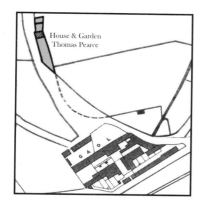

has been produced from the Bodmin Town and Bodmin Borough Tithe maps.) It also clearly shows the angular section of the front wall. The darker coloured building and the building to the right of it are the Governor's House and the Infirmary block from the original gaol. Many of the extended and new buildings are in the same relative positions as those shown on the Tithe map plan. This painting is a three-dimensional representation of the gaol in 1840-41. However there may be a problem with the date as there was no recorded execution at Bodmin in 1841.

There is a sketch of the execution of Benjamin Ellison at Bodmin in 1845, published in a broadsheet by E. Keys of Devonport.[19] Is it an authentic picture of Bodmin Gaol?

The gatehouse and walls are shown as castellated, quite different to the 1841 picture, and part of the wall has been replaced by a cottage. There are two possible explanations for these changes, either the castellation and cottages were built during the 1842 building programme or, more likely, the Artist had never seen Bodmin Gaol.

It is very sad that the beautiful original 1779 Georgian buildings had become the totally unplanned random collection of buildings shown in the 1840 map and 1841 painting. The original designers could not have foreseen the increase in population, the resulting crime wave and increase in prison population but there must have been other factors which resulted in some of the changes. The addition of the workshop and 'Vagrant Ward for Boys' were very early changes, closely followed by the stopping up of the arcades in 1780. This would indicate that the original plan was very idealistic and elegant but it did not fulfil the function of a gaol.

In the mid 1850s the 'old gaol' was abandoned a new gaol was built.

Bodmin Gaol, 1894.

(F.G.Stone Collection)

Bodmin Gaol, about 1900.

(F.G.Stone Collection)

CHAPTER 4

The New Bodmin Gaol

It was noted in the Governor's and Chaplain's Report of October 1854 that overcrowding in the gaol had encouraged association of prisoners.[16] The total separation of different types of prisoners, sexes and individuals, who were not allowed to communicate, even when working together, was one of the main principals of the John Howard proposals for prison reform. The themes of separation and silence had been reinforced in Robert Peel's Gaol Act of 1823 [20] and were still in favour in the 1850s. The separation of prisoners was probably more important to the Authorities than the dilapidated state of the gaol and the overcrowding.

In 1855, the Visiting Justices Report on the building of a new County Gaol stated that plans should be produced for a new gaol to accommodate the maximum numbers of prisoners. £25,000 was allocated by the County Authorities. The architect of the building was a Mr F W Porter of London and the gaol was to be built on the same site at Berrycombe but using the old gaol site, the gaol gardens and other pieces of adjacent land. Initial quotations for the work were all significantly over the £25,000 available. The plans were modified and by using less granite and cheaper materials, a new lower estimate of £26,650 was obtained from Goodyear and King of Devon.[21] This quotation did not include fittings, gas and water services or architects fees. The final cost of the building was reported in *The Royal Cornwall Gazette* as "upwards of forty thousand pounds". The building started in 1857 but the strategy of housing the prisoners during the building of the new gaol is not clear. In 1861 [22], the 26th Report of the Inspectors of Prisons', contained the following statement:

> The reconstruction of this prison was rapidly advancing towards completion at the time of my last inspection on the 11th September last *(1860)*. At the end of the year 1859, I had the satisfaction of certifying 141 cells for the adoption of separate confinement in a wing which will eventually be devoted to male prisoners, a part of which is however now used by prisoners of the other sex during the erection of their proper building.

The new gaol was built of stone from Cuckoo *Quarry (Gaol Quarry as shown on the tithe map)* until it was exhausted. Additional material was bought by tender. It had been suggested that stone from the old buildings should be reused in the new buildings to save money but this idea proved impractical because of the poor quality of the stone recovered. The old gaol was finally removed by a contractor at a cost of £50.

Labour was not a problem as quarrying just became another form of hard labour. Perhaps the prisoners enjoyed the new task as it gave them the opportunity to work outside the prison. However this practice was criticised by the Inspectors:

> The inclination of the ground upon which the prison is erected, formerly the site of that which it has superseded, is so steep that much excavation and levelling will be necessary to obtain convenient airing yards at the back of the prison which will be safe against escape, and not overlooked from the surrounding country. **This was in progress at the time of my visit and was being carried on entirely by prisoners, some of whom were also employed, in a manner less to be commended, without the walls of the prison. Granting the desirableness of saving to the county the expense of hired labour in the performance of works on the exterior of the prison, I cannot admit the propriety of the practice of taking out the prisoners for that purpose, whatever may be the care and discrimination with which they may be selected for the duty.**

The new gaol was officially opened in 1859. The male block was occupied shortly after that and the female block was completed in 1860.

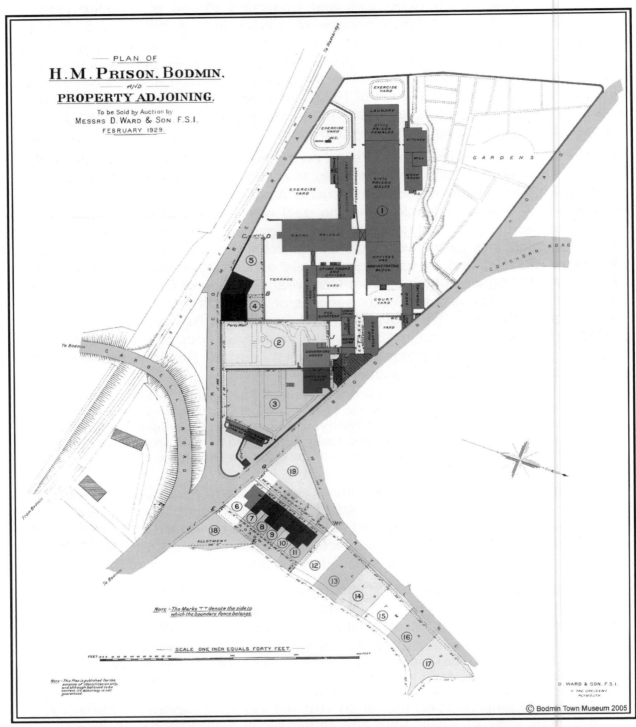

Plan of H. M. Prison, Bodmin from the Sale Document, 1929.

Description of gaol (1929)

No original plans of the site have been found but there is general agreement that the gaol changed very little between 1860 and its sale in 1929. The sale documents, prepared by Messrs. D. Ward and Son of Plymouth,[23] contain a full plan of the gaol, the adjoining properties and a detailed description of each of the buildings on the site.

From the plan, the gaol consisted of the following buildings. The main civil prison block contained four separate sections: offices, prison administration and chapel; male prison; female prison; and laundry. The Naval Prison block was joined to the main block at the first and second floor levels. A building, linked to the Naval Prison by covered walkway on the first floor, contained: store rooms; offices and naval administration; and a naval infirmary. The kitchen, mill and workroom block of the civil prison. A kitchen and laundry attached to the Naval Prison. The main gateway and staff quarters, stables and the execution shed. Two houses for the Chief and Principal Officers. The houses for the Governor and chaplain were outside the prison. The sale document contained the following details of the buildings.

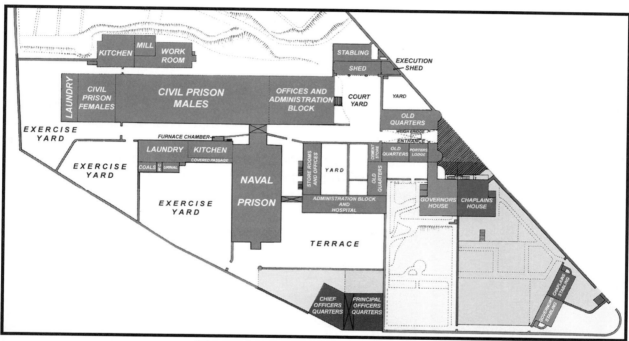

Plan of the Gaol Buildings 1929.

Main Gateway and Staff Quarters

This building forms the main entrance to the gaol and is still used today. Through the archway can be seen the original double storey staff quarters, which were removed after the sale in 1930. Opposite these quarters is a similar block, which contained the gatekeepers lodge and more staff quarters, which is still in use.

Originally the area between the two sets of quarters was kept secure by two sets of gates. The outside gates are shown in the photograph. The other pair of gates, at the end of the two staff blocks, was made of iron. It is believed locally that these gates were sold and used at the Apex Garage in Scorrier but those gates were very ornate for a Victorian prison. The gates at the garage have been reported to come from Tehidy, Cornwall and not Bodmin Gaol.[24] Recently, the site of the inner gates has been unearthed. The gates were 48in. wide and each had a 2in. wheel or roller to enable easier opening and closing.

The Main Block (Administration section)

This was the largest building on the site. Viewed from the gatehouse the first part of the block was used for administration and offices on the ground/first floor. Above this

was the chapel and on the third floor were storage space and the access to the turret. There was also a large basement, which extended under the male prison. In the link between the administration section and the male prison on the ground/first floor was the large condemned cell with the iron gates.

The Main Block (Male Civil Prison)

The prison was on four floors. The ground floor area was 6,700 square feet. The lowest floor contained offices, bathrooms, a kitchen etc. together with 16 cells and a punishment cell fitted with iron gates. The ground/first floor contained 31 cells and the

top two floors, each had 33 cells. These floors had slate slab galleries supported on steel girders and protected by iron railings. The floors were connected by a circular stone stairway. All the cell doors were 6ft 3in x 2ft 3in and 2½ inches thick. They were lined internally with iron. This part of the prison had a total of 114 cells. There was a lift to take food from the basement to the cells.

There is an extra area below ground which was probably the boiler room and coal storage area.

The Main Block (Female Prison)

The third section of the main block was for women prisoners. In general, it was similar to the male prison. It was on four floors and had galleries on the top two floors and the same size cells. There were 31 cells, arranged with seven on the lowest floor and eight on each of the other three floors. The ground floor area was 2,000 square feet.

The Main Block (Laundry)

This was a single storey with a floor area of 700 square feet. It contained five washing cubicles, each fitted with washing trays and water supply and a bathroom with a boiler.

Kitchen, Mill and Workroom

The kitchen covered an area of 810 square feet had a 60ft high chimney stack and was fitted with skylights. The workroom and mill, area 1,400 square feet, had wooden flooring and a lavatory. It is not known when this kitchen replaced the one in the main building.

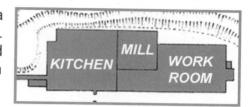

Naval Prison Block

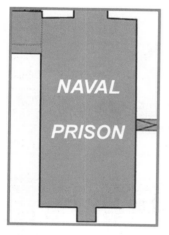

The 1929 sale document describes the Naval Prison as having five floors with a ground floor area of 4,600 square feet. The ground floor had 18 cells (13 feet x 7 feet), the first floor 21 cells and a gallery of slate slabs, supported on iron beams and protected with iron railings. The second, third and fourth floors each with 22 cells.

Naval Administration Block and Infirmary

This building is approached from the Naval Prison by overhead passage and covers an area of 2,150 square feet. It has three floors and a large basement. These premises are connected to store rooms and offices covering an area of 825 square feet, which together form two sides of an enclosed yard.

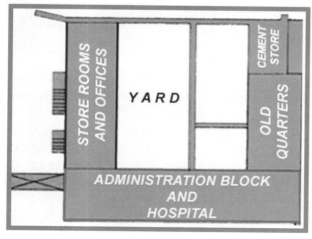

Kitchen and Laundry (Naval Prison)

This block connected to the Naval Prison contained: kitchen, floor area 900 square feet, with slate flooring; two bathrooms and a laundry, area 1,100 square feet, which contained copper furnace and boiler. The picture also shows the coal store.

Naval Officers Houses, Governor's House and Chaplaincy

In 1892, two villas were built to house the Chief Officer and the Principal Officer of

the Naval prison. In 1929, they were sold as private houses as were the Chaplaincy and the Governor's House. These properties are still privately owned.

Stables and Shed

The stables contained six stalls with wooden partitions, mangers and iron racks, together with an open shed. Total floor area 950 square feet. In the 1890s, the right hand side of the shed was converted into an execution shed.

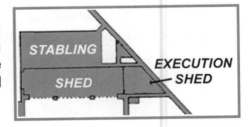

Recorded Changes to the Buildings between 1860 and 1929

In addition to the detailed description of the buildings in 1929, there are published photographs dating from the turn of the twentieth century, which show most of the main buildings and the walls. The details are generally consistent with the later plan but there are differences. Firstly, in the 1894 picture, there is a small building or shed, in the South-East corner of the Naval prison exercise yard. No details of this building have been found but it must have been demolished before ca.1900.

The second difference is an extension at the southern end of the Naval Prison block to give an extra 30 cells in 1901. The photograph, which is dated ca.1900, shows building work on the southern end of the naval block. The poor quality picture shows scaffolding, many pieces of stone, a ladder and a man building a new wall. It would suggest that the extension was built with the granite quoins being removed from the main building as the wall was increased. The quoins were then used to make the corners of the extension. The outside shell was built and secured before

the original end wall was removed. By this strategy the prisoners could remain inside a secure building.

Other changes are the building of the Officers quarters (Naval Villas) in 1892 and the execution shed.

Recorded Change in Use of the Buildings between 1860 and 1929

The major change was the transfer of two of the main blocks from the County Gaol to the Naval Prison Authorities. The number of prisoners in the gaol had been falling and the gaol had occasionally been used to house naval prisoners from about 1855. In 1873, problems at Devonport forced the Admiralty to send increased numbers of prisoners to Bodmin. In 1887, two prison blocks, which had been used to house female prisoners and debtors, were handed over to the naval authorities. From this date the gaol was administered by both civil and naval authorities.

The change in use is reflected in an analysis of the number and use of prison cells.

Number of Cells in each Section of the Gaol									
Year	M	F	Punish. (M & F)	Recept. (M & F)	Civil Total	Debtors	Naval	Total	Ref.
1855	150	50	6 + 2	?	208	?		208+	25
1866	141	59	6 + 2	7 + 5	220	25 + 4 day rooms		249	26
1889					129		75	204	27
1906					129		105	234	28
1929	114	31			145		105	250	23

The original plan of the gaol was for 200 cells of which 50 were for females and an additional 8 punishment cells (6M and 2F). When the gaol was completed, the total number of cells had increased to 249 or 250. (It is not known whether the condemned cell is included in all the different reports.) The data from the 31st Report on Prisons (1866) gives the most detailed accommodation data: 141 male cells, 59 female cells, 8 (6M + 2F) punishment cells and 12 (7M & 5F) reception cells. It also contains 25 debtors sleeping cells, including 5 for females, and 4 dayrooms, 2 for each sex. These numbers are also included in the 39th Report (1875) [29] and the 42nd Report of 1878.[30] Kelly's Directories of Cornwall up to 1887 give a total figure of 250 cells.

The Kelly's Directory of Cornwall, 1889, shows the loss of the debtor's cells and dayrooms and a total cell number reduced from 250 to 204, that is, 75 naval cells and 129 civil cells. As the total number of cells should be 220, there are 16 cells missing. When the gaol was sold the number of cells in the civil block is reported as 145. The 16 cells have reappeared. It seems likely that when the gaol split into two, the basement of the main block, which contained 16 cells, was taken out of use and maybe used for storage.

What were the two buildings, which became the naval block and the naval administration / infirmary ward, used for before the change?

From the shape of the infirmary building with its court yard, this was the Debtor's prison. From the numbers of males and female cells, it seems likely that the Naval Prison was originally the female prison block. The block was built to house 59 females plus 2 punishment cells, 5 reception cells, bathrooms and workrooms. This block was later used to accommodate 75 naval prisoners. This separate block for females was consistent with the principle of separation of the sexes in vogue at the time. It was also reported that during the building of the gaol, women were housed in the male block while the women's block was completed.

When the females were moved into the main building in 1887, a new wall must have been built to separate the male and female prisoners. The original laundry was next to the women's block and the single story new laundry building at the end of the main block was probably added after 1887.

The following diagram summarises the use of the buildings before and after 1887.

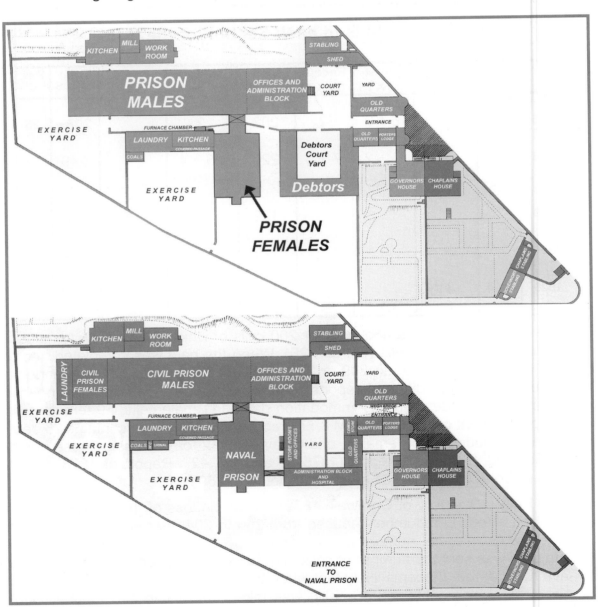

CHAPTER 5

Position of the Old Gaol

Although the old gaol was built on the same site as the new gaol, its position in relation to the later buildings is not recorded. In an attempt to position the original buildings the following documents have been used:

1. Ground plan of gaol from the Call Engraving (page 14).[8] This plan is to scale.
2. Bodmin Town & Bodmin Borough Tithe maps, 1840.[17] Hand drawn buildings.
3. 'Plan and Sections of the proposed Alteration of Roads for the enlargement of the County Gaol, Bodmin, Cornwall'.[31] Architect's drawing.
4. Ordinance Survey map, 1881.[32] This map contains only the outline of the boundary of the gaol.
5. The Sale Document plan, 1929.[23] Architect's drawing (page 24).
6. Ordinance Survey map,1970.[33]

Documents 1 to 5 were digitised, edited, scaled and overlaid. The gaol boundary walls on the documents 4, 5 & 6 are identical. The walls had not changed from before 1881 until many years after the gaol was closed. It is possible that the walls shown in the 1881 plan are the original 1859 walls as the 1853 document is only a proposal and not an agreed plan.

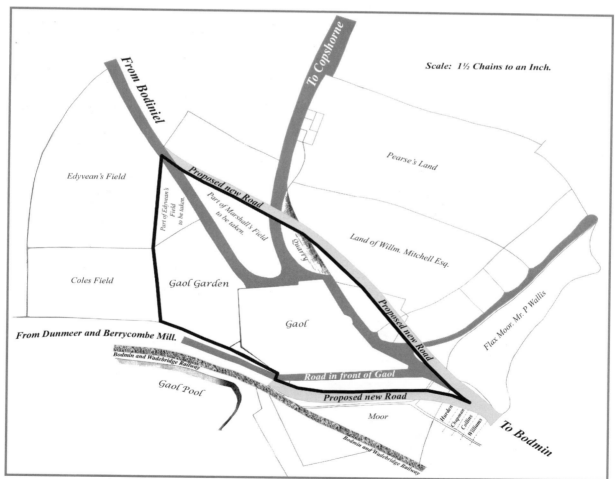

Document 3 (1853): Showing the outline of the old gaol, the position of the old roads (dark grey), proposed new roads (light grey) and the new wall (black)

The key step in finding the site of the old gaol was to fix the position of *'the road in front of the gaol'* onto the 1929 document and to confirm that the *'Proposed new road'* was in the same place in 1853 & 1929.

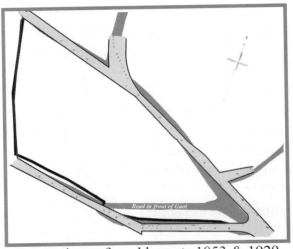

Comparison of road layouts 1853 & 1929

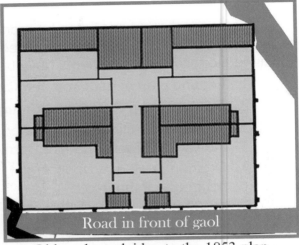

Old gaol overlaid onto the 1853 plan

The new roads show some differences to the original proposals. The main change is in the curved corner at the bottom right of the diagram in place of the strange pointed feature. Bodiniel Road is straighter than in the proposal but the junctions are in the same places. This overlay now allows the *'road in front of the gaol'*, and therefore the old gaol, to be fixed onto the 1929 sale document plan.

In addition, the 1779 gaol, which was 172 ft. wide by 144 ft., fits the 1853 road plan, including the small portion which extends into the road. Both of these plans are to scale.

The diagram below shows both the position of the old gaol on the 1929 sale plan and the great increase in the gaol area between 1779 and 1929.

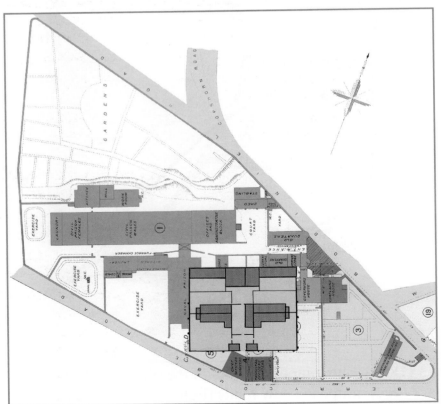

The Position of the Original Gaol

EXECUTION SHED

STABLING

SHED

YARD

OLD QUARTERS

COURT YARD

OFFICES AND ADMINISTRATION BLOCK

WEIGH BRIDGE

ENTRANCE

OLD QUARTERS

PORTERS LODGE

CEMENT STORE

GOVERNORS HOUSE

CHAPLAINS HOUSE

GOVERNORS STABLING

CHAPLAINS STABLING

OLD QUAR

ADMINISTRATION BLOCK AND HOSPITAL

STORE ROOMS AN

PRINCIPAL OFFICERS QUARTERS

CHIEF OFFICERS QUARTERS

NAVAL PRISON

CIVIL PRISON MALES

MILL

KITCHEN

WORK ROOM

CIVIL PRISON FEMALES

LAUNDRY

FURNACE CHAMBER

LAUNDRY

KITCHEN

COVERED PASSAGE

COALS

W C

URINAL

EXERCISE YARD

EXERCISE YARD

EXERCISE YARD

EXERCISE YARD

This diagram is an edited version of the previous overlay.

It shows the buildings and walls of the old gaol in relationship to the buildings present in 1929.

The Position of the Extended Gaol

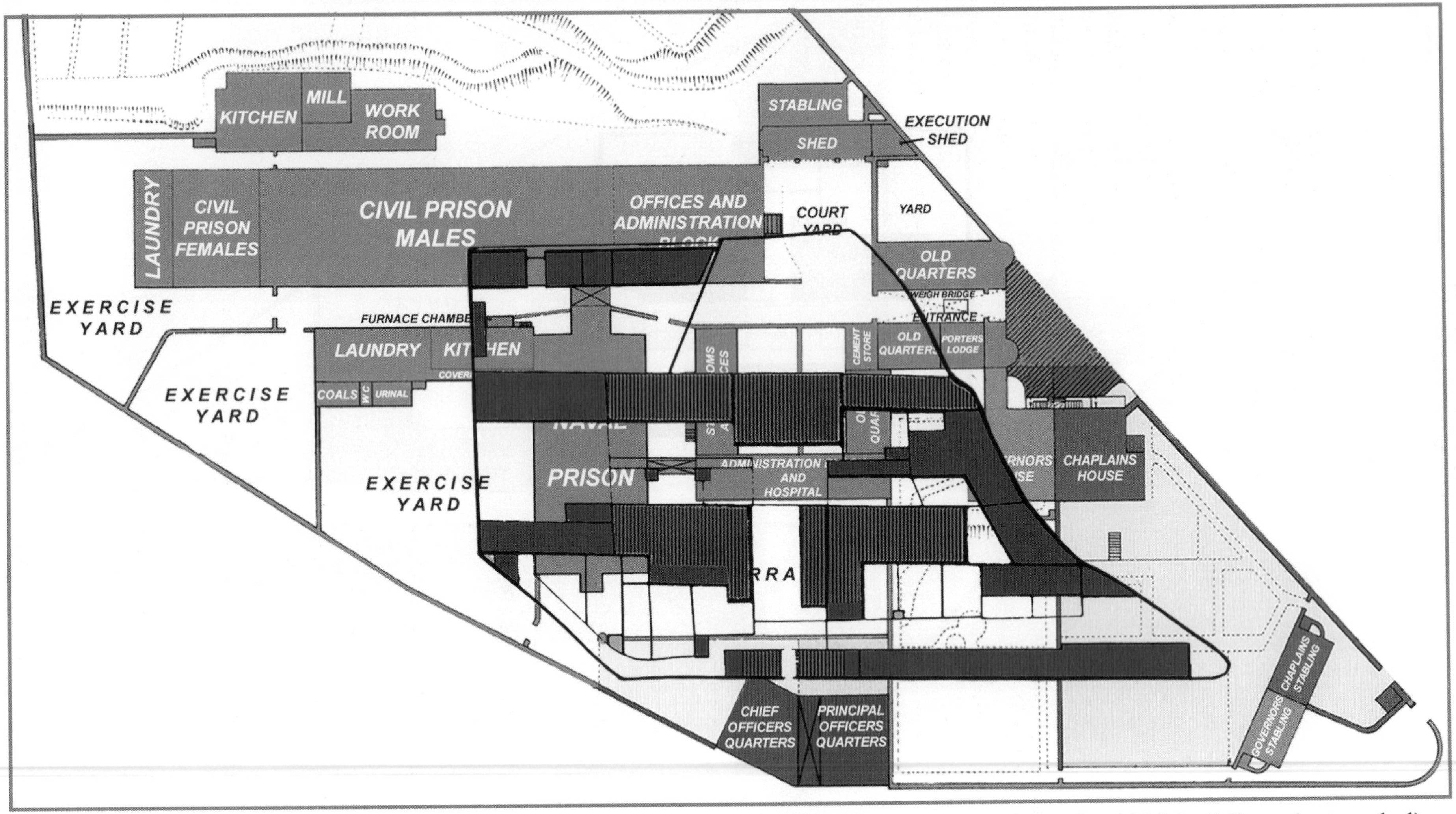

This diagram shows the approximate position of the 1840 extended gaol in relationship to the 1929 buildings (not scaled)

Labels within the diagram:

- EXECUTION SHED
- STABLING
- SHED
- YARD
- OLD QUARTERS
- WEIGH BRIDGE
- ENTRANCE
- OLD PORTERS LODGE
- OLD QUARTERS
- CEMENT STORE
- COURT YARD
- OFFICES AND ADMINISTRATION BLOCK
- CIVIL PRISON MALES
- FURNACE CHAMBER
- LAUNDRY KITCHEN
- COALS
- W C URINAL
- MILL
- WORK ROOM
- KITCHEN
- CIVIL PRISON FEMALES
- LAUNDRY
- EXERCISE YARD
- EXERCISE YARD
- EXERCISE YARD
- EXERCISE YARD
- NAVAL PRISON
- ADMINISTRATION AND HOSPITAL
- CHAPLAINS HOUSE
- GOVERNORS HOUSE
- CHAPLAINS STABLING
- GOVERNORS STABLING
- PRINCIPAL OFFICERS QUARTERS
- CHIEF OFFICERS QUARTERS
- STORE ROOMS

CHAPTER 6

English Gaol Administration

For most of the eighteenth century no one cared very much about what happened to felons. Many were hanged, thrown into dungeons or transported to work in the American plantations. The American War of Independence (1778 -1783) put an end to the transportation and the government had to provide accommodation for about 1,000 convicts per year. The simple solution was to house the convicts in the ships previously used as transports. They were moored in places like Portsmouth, Chatham and London and the prisoners were employed on local public works. Planned as a temporary measure, the use of prison hulks lasted until 1858. The Government's stated intention was to build new prisons and there was much discussion of the reformist ideas of Howard after the publication of his book in 1777. Some of the Howard principles were included in Sir William Blackstone's Penitentiary Act of 1779,[34] and the further Acts of 1782 and 1784.[35,36] These Acts all failed as there were no new prisons built and the old places of detention were in no state to be converted into the new Howard type establishments. The Prison Act of 1791,[37] which stated that the principles of cellular confinement and enforced silence, both mentioned in the earlier Acts, should apply to all prisons. However, the Act was not compulsory and no inspection system was initiated. This Act was largely ignored. From 1791 to 1815 the country was too involved in the Napoleonic Wars to worry about convicts. The hulks were still in use and, after 1787, convicts were now transported to Australia. These solutions to the prisoner problem were much cheaper than building expensive new prisons.

After the war, with an increasing gaol population, conditions in gaols moved higher up the agenda. In 1815,[38] all prison fees were abolished and exacting money from prisoners became a penal offence but there was no inspection to see that the new measures were effective. In 1823 Peel, then Home Secretary, introduced and passed the 'The Gaol Act'.[20] This was largely a consolidating act, reaffirming the four Howard principles which had previously been enacted and neglected in 1779 and 1791:

1. Provision of secure, roomy and sanitary prisons.
2. Change gaoler from profit-maker into a salaried public servant.
3. Subjection of prisoners to a reformatory regime of diet, work and religious exercises.
4. Systematic inspection of the prison by outside public authority.

The objectives of the Act were 'effectively to preserve the health and improve the morals of the prisoners as well as to ensure the proper punishment to convicted offenders'. The Act included the following Rules and Regulations:

i) The male & female prisoners shall be confined in separate buildings, so as to prevent them from seeing or conversing with each other.

ii) The prisoners of each sex shall be divided into distinct classes, care being taken that when at labour they only associate with other members of the same class:

In Gaols:

1st	Debtors/ contempt of court or civil process
2nd	Convicted of Felony
3rd	Convicted of Misdemeanours
4th	Charged with Felony
5th	Charged with Misdemeanours or for Want of Sureties

In Houses of Correction (formerly Bridewells):

1st	Convicted of Felony
2nd	Convicted of Misdemeanours
3rd	Charged with Felony
4th	Charged with Misdemeanours
5th	Vagrants

These are the same classifications, which were used in the design of the Bodmin Gaol, with the addition of vagrants and the separation of prisoners charged with a crime and those convicted.

iii)   Female supervision of female prisoners

iv)   Gaolers, surgeons and chaplains must inspect the prison at regular intervals, keep records and to present them to the justices at the Quarter Sessions. The justices must then report to the Home Secretary

v)   Dietaries.

This Act only applied to prisons under the control of the justices. Some 150 others, used largely for the confinement of debtors, were unaffected. The main weakness of the Act was that there was no provision for inspectors. The Home Office demanded of the justices a certain standard but the only reports required by law were from the justices themselves.

In a further attempt to get uniformity of punishments and conditions in all gaols, a further Act was passed in 1835,[39] which allowed the appointment of five 'Inspectors of Prisons', who visited all gaols and reported directly to the government. The inspectors were allowed to give advice to the local authorities but they had no power to enforce the provisions of Peel's 1823 Act.

From about this time, there was a tendency toward the 'separate system', not only for different types of prisoners but for individuals. The idea was that a prisoner was confined to a cell, which was his workshop by day and his bedroom by night. This prevented prisoners talking, or even being recognised by each other. It was believed that continuous solitude would result in the reformation of the prisoner but in practice it often resulted in the prisoner's insanity. The Prisons Act of 1839[40] provided for *'individual separation of prisoners during the whole or any part of their imprisonment and that this separation shall not be deemed solitary confinement.'*

In 1863, deficiencies in the local administration of gaols were catalogued by a Select Committee of the House of Lords. This led to the Prison Act of 1865,[41] which was the last great measure for penal administration while the prisons were under local control. The Act, which covered all aspects of prison life, contains 82 clauses and three Schedules containing a further 104 regulations, a list of prisons to be closed and a list of 18 Acts to be wholly or partially repealed, including those mentioned above. It was the final attempt by central government to unify the prison system and included the following provisions:-

i)   All difference between gaols & houses of correction *(formerly bridewells used for Misdemeanours)* were abolished.

ii)   Justices still retained control but now under strict control from headquarters.

iii)   Justices must build prisons according to government plans.

iv)   Penal labour must be in defined form.

v)   Dietaries must be submitted to the Home Office.

vi)   New code of prison regulations.

vii)   New classifications for Hard Labour class 1 and 2.

viii)   Government powers to close inadequate local gaols. *(For Cornwall, this meant the closure of the local gaols in Falmouth, Penzance and Helstone by the 1st February, 1866.)* [26]

ix)   Every local prison should have separate cells equal to the average greatest number of prisoners held at any time in the previous five years.

Four years later an Act to abolish prison for debtors was passed.[42] This Act came into operation on the same day as the 'Bankruptcy Act' 1869'.[43] Debtors could still go to prison for defaulting on a court settlement or for fraud in a bankruptcy settlement. Leaving England with over £20 after being declared bankrupt was a felony carrying a sentence of two years. Before this Act, creditors could have their debtors imprisoned under 'The Lords' Act of 1759' and should have provided the debtor with 4d. per day allowance (groats) but this was rarely paid.

Even with all the above Acts of Parliament, the government was still not convinced that a truly uniform prison system existed in England. So they enacted the 1877 Prison Act [44] which resulted in the total nationalisation of the prison system and transferred all aspects of prison administration, including the costs, to the Secretary of State and the Prison Commissioners from the local justices. Bodmin Gaol ceased to be the County Gaol and became H M Prison, Bodmin.

The final Act of Parliament enacted during the life-time of the gaol, was the Prison Act of 1898.[45] In addition to changes in the employment of prisoners, a new classification of prisoners was introduced. This consisted of three divisions and was intended to prevent contamination of low level prisoners by 'those who are depraved or of criminal habits':

First Division: Intended for strictly limited classes of prisoners, for example, those committed of contempt of court or offences loosely described as 'political'. This division was non-punitive and as reasonably comfortable that the conditions of prison life and discipline would allow.

Second Division: For prisoners, who in the opinion of the court should be separated from hardened criminals.

Third Division: All prisoners who were not in the above divisions.

Unlike earlier Acts, the work and general treatment of the prisoners in the 2nd and 3rd Divisions, were identical.

Against the national background of no new prison buildings and the use of hulks and transportation, the Justices in Cornwall, had totally accepted Howard's reforms and had built the new gaol in Bodmin to his designs. The gaol was probably the only prison which was able to comply with the Acts of Parliament and all the government's stated ideals up to the start of the nineteenth century. Later, the Justices enforced all the Acts of Parliament. After the Peel Act, they planned the big expansion of the gaol to allow the 'separation system' to be implemented and issued new Rules & Regulations from the Act. Changes in the treatment of prisoners including employment, diets, prison offences and punishments always resulted after new legislation.

Bodmin Town Museum

Henry Leonard Browett
Last Governor of H M Prison, Bodmin

Richard Amos Doidge (1860-1945)
Chief Warder, H M Prison, Bodmin.

Service Medal awarded to
Richard A. Doidge

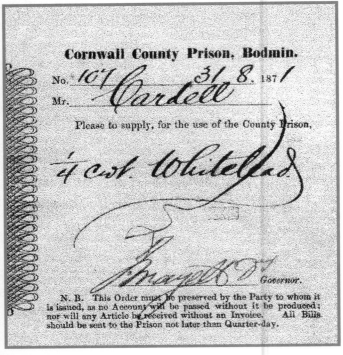

Order Signed by James Mayell
Principal Warder, 1871
Bodmin Town Museum

CHAPTER 7

Crimes and Sentences

In the early 19th century, before the police force was formed in 1856, any person suspected of a crime was taken by the parish constable or the person who caught the suspect, to the magistrate. He could release the person, or if he had committed a minor **'summary offence'**, for example, poaching or vagrancy, he could be tried on the spot by the magistrate and sent to gaol, or he could be sent to the Petty Sessions, a court consisting of two magistrates with no jury. If the magistrate thought that the offence was indictable, the prisoner would be sent to gaol until the next Quarter Sessions or, for the most serious crimes, to the Assizes. Feloniously stealing cases went to the Quarter Sessions or the Assizes depending on the value of the stolen goods. If the goods stolen from a shop were valued at over 5 shillings or from a house forty shillings, the criminal was tried at the Assizes and faced the death penalty.

Quarter Sessions

The Quarter Sessions dealt with the crimes of assault, bastardy, felony, vagrancy, including begging, receiving stolen goods, keeping a disorderly house and taking money or goods by false pretences.

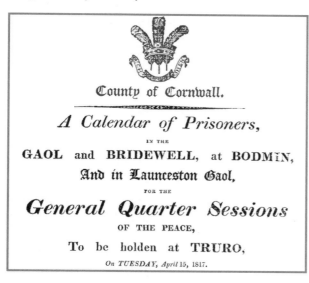

County of Cornwall.

A Calendar of Prisoners,

IN THE

GAOL and BRIDEWELL, at BODMIN,

And in Launceston Gaol,

FOR THE

General Quarter Sessions

OF THE PEACE,

To be holden at TRURO,

On TUESDAY, April 15, 1817.

The Calendar for the Quarter Sessions, April 15, 1817[46] contains the following trials: **Bastardy,** (19 cases), including John Trevail, committed October 21, 1815, for Want of Sureties to indemnify the Parish of Buryan, in Bastardy. This was a crime for men who had fathered an illegitimate child or women who would not name the father. They were imprisoned until they could guarantee, by way of sureties, to indemnify the local parish for supporting the child; **Vagrancy** (10), for example, Elizabeth Worsdell, committed February 9, 1817, as a lewd, idle, disorderly person, wandering in the Parish of Redruth; **Felony** (10), Richard Halliggy, charged with stealing three geese; **Assault** (8), John Bishop, committed for Want of Sureties in a Breach of the Peace committed against Martha his wife.

Assizes

The quarterly Assizes dealt with the more serious crimes of burglary, felony, fraud and murder. Typical examples of the crimes tried at the Assizes are contained in the Calendar of Prisoners for the Assizes, 8th August, 1803.[47]

Prisoners in Bodmin Gaol, on former Orders:

Mary Salt (24) convicted of Felony, Summer Assizes, 1801. Sentence: Death - Pardoned on Condition of being transported for Life

Rose Harris (49) convicted of Sheep Stealing, Lent Assizes, 1803. Sentence: Death - Pardoned on Condition of being transported for Life

Elizabeth Collins (42) convicted of Grand Larceny, Lent Assizes, 1803. Sentence: To be kept to hard labour in the House of Correction 12 months.

Prisoners for Trial in Bodmin Gaol:

1. Henry Dower (28), charged with having burglariously broken and entered the Dwelling House of Reuben Magor, of Redruth and stealing one Silver Milk Cup and sundry other Articles. Again charged with having burglariously broken and entered the Dwelling House of Charles Reed, silversmith, of the Borough of Helston and stealing one Gold Ring and sundry other Articles. Again charged with having burglariously broken and entered the Shop of Jacob Jacob, Watchmaker, and stolen one square Barrel Gun, several Watch Seals, and sundry other Articles.

2. Peter Dowd (26) charged with having uttered (put into circulation) several Counterfeit shillings, as and for the legal current Coin of this Realm.

3. Richard Hawken (19), charged with stealing a Watch, the Property of Walter Ratty, and also on Suspicion of breaking into the house of Catherine Ratty, and stealing from thence sundry Articles.

4. Jane Carllen (44), charged with having received into her Custody, a male Bastard Child, which she deserted and left exposed in a Cart, and which afterwards died.

Cornwall

A Calendar of the Prisoners,

In the GAOLS of the said COUNTY,

Remaining on former ORDERS, and for TRIAL,

AT THE

SUMMER ASSIZES,

TO BE HELD AT

B O D M I N,

On M O N D A Y, the 8th of AUGUST, 1808,

BEFORE

The Right Honorable

RICHARD PEPPER ARDEN, LORD ALVANLEY,

Chief Justice of our Lord the King, of his Court of Common Pleas,

AND

SIR ROBERT GRAHAM, KNIGHT,

One of the Barons of our said Lord the King, of his Court of Exchequer.

THOMAS RAWLINGS, ESQ.

S H E R I F F.

Prisoners in BODMIN GAOL, on former Orders.

Name.	Age.	When convicted	What Offence.	Sentence.
Mary Salt,	24	Summer Affizes 1801.	Felony.	Death—Pardoned on Condition of being tranfported for Life Ditto.
Rofe Harris,	49	Lent Affizes, 1803.	Sheep Stealing.	Ditto.
Elizabeth Collins,	41	Ditto.	Grand Larceny.	To be kept to hard Labor in the Houfe of Correction 12 Months.

BODMIN : *Printed by* JAMES LIDDELL, *Printer and Book-binder.*

5. William Stevens (49), charged with maliciously and feloniously stabbing and killing two Heifers, the Property of Richard Morris.

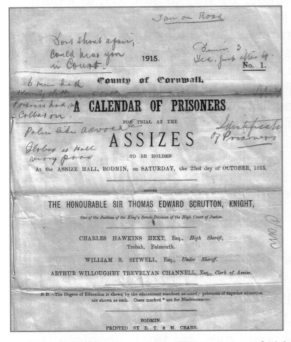

In line with the increase in crime during the middle of the 19th century, the Calendar of Prisoners for Trial at the Assizes at Bodmin, 16th March, 1869,[48] lists 41 cases. The crimes were: **stealing** (27), **breaking & entering** (3), **'endeavouring to conceal the birth of a child and disposing of the dead body'** (3), **embezzlement** (2) and one case of each of the following: **forgery, killing, infanticide, receiving stolen goods, violent assault & feloniously ravishing and wounding** with grievous bodily harm.

In the 20th century, the number of Assize cases decreased. Three of the Calendars[49] for 1914 contain a total of 28 cases, much less than the one Calendar for 1869. The Calendar for 23rd October, 1915, probably the last Assizes before the closure of the gaol, contains a list of twelve cases. The copy of this document held in Bodmin Town Museum, has been annotated with the outcome of the trials and the sentences.

Calendar of Prisoners for Trial at Assizes, Bodmin on 23rd. October, 1915.

No.	NAME, AGE AND TRADE.	Particulars of Offence	Sentence
	PRISONERS FOR TRIAL		
1	George Martin, 40, Soldier	At Falmouth, on the 3rd June, 1915, did feloniously forge a Banker's Cheque for the payment of £2 with intent to defraud. Also Committed:-	Bound over for 12 months in £5.
2	Alfred Smith, 38, Soldier	At Falmouth, on the 5th June, 1915, did feloniously forge a Banker's Cheque for the payment of £1-10-0 with intent to defraud.	Bound over for 12 months in £5.
3	Stephen Henry Stratton, 48, Soldier	At Trewen, on the 16th June, 1913, did feloniously marry Frances Caroline Allen, his former wife, Henrietta Rosetta, to whom he was previously married, being then alive.	3 years Penal Servitude
4	Alfred Vellanoweth, 16, Labourer	At Camborne, on the 25th June, 1915, did unlawfully assault with intent to feloniously ravish and carnally know, against her will, Olive Pearce.	Bound over for 12 months in £5.
5	Frederick Taylor, 25, Labourer	At Poundstock, on the 29th June, 1915, did feloniously set fire to a stack of oat and barley straw, the property of James Trathen.	
6	William Alfred Bray, 24, Labourer	At St. Stephens-in-Bramwell, on the 2nd July, 1915, did unlawfully and carnally know Hilda Ann Trethewey, she being a girl above the age of 13 years and under the age of 16 years.	Not Guilty
7	Arthur Edward Heath, 34, Agent	At Camborne on the 6th May, 1915, being entrusted by the National Amalgamated Approved Society with the sum of ten shillings for payment to Andrew Hocking, did unlawfully and fraudulently convert the sum of five shillings, part thereof, to his own use and benefit.	Bound over for 12 months in £5.
8	William Brailsford, 31, Miner	At Gwennap, on the 11th August, 1915, did feloniously and maliciously wound Albina Brailsford with intent to do her some grievous bodily harm.	12 months
9	Annie Ethel Jenkin, 21, Servant	At Bodmin, on the 22nd May, 1915 did feloniously, forge a cheque for £3 purporting to be signed by A. S. Lund and drawn on the Capital and Counties Bank, Bodmin, with intent to defraud.	6 months (2nd Division)
10	Gordon Abel, 19, Labourer	At Mabe, on the 3rd October, 1915, did feloniously break and enter the shop of Mary Jane Williams and steal the sum of 2s. 5d., also 4 packets of cigarettes; 3 collar studs and some roll tobacco, the monies and goods of Mary Jane Williams.	Bound over for 12 months in £5.
11	Mads Peter Mortensen, 22, Captain's Mate	At St. Blazey, on the 16th September, 1915, did feloniously and maliciously wound, with a knife, and break the leg of Frank Louis Pittaway, with intent to do him some grievous bodily harm.	
12	John Nathaniel Lewis, 45, Seaman		

Convictions, Sentences and Other Punishments

The Quarter Sessions records, showing the indictments and sentences, for the years 1812, 1822 and 1832 are collated in Appendix 2. The cases listed in these records are mainly for taking, later called stealing, and there are a few other crimes, including begging, keeping a disorderly house, vagrancy, false pretences and assault.

1812: (13 cases) There were 11 convictions for stealing. The punishments handed down by the Court do not appear to relate to the seriousness of the crime or the value of the goods stolen. Richard Chipas stole 12 apples and received one week in gaol, Thomas Reed, who stole a brass pan and a fowling piece, two separate crimes, was sentenced to three months hard labour and a public whipping *'for 100 yards up the street in Bodmin'* but John Chapman, who stole one gallon of wheat, was sentenced to two years hard labour, during which time on two market days, public whipping in streets of Bodmin *'from Butter Market 100 yards up the street unless he shall in the meantime voluntarily enter into his Majesty's army.'* Sixty percent of the men and two of the three women were sentenced with hard labour. Three men received whippings.

1822: (47 cases) There were two acquittals, one male & one female. Fourteen men were whipped (some of the whippings were now private) and 50% sentenced to hard labour as were two of the nine women.

1832: (107 cases) There were 104 convictions and three acquittals (2M & 1F). There were only 5 private whippings, but the number of prisoners sentenced to hard labour, ninety-three percent of men and eighty-six percent of women, show a great increase from earlier years. One prisoner was transported.

The Inspectors of Prisons Reports contain the following information:

1843: (Convictions 503) The average time from arrest to trial was 10 weeks but 6 prisoners waited over 6 months. The average sentence for those under summary conviction was 10 weeks. There were additional punishments handed down by the Courts. There were 12 private whippings and 10 prisoners sentenced to solitary confinement. Forty percent of the prisoners were employed at hard labour. Transportation had become more popular with the Judges and 29 prisoners were transported for times ranging from 7 years to life.

1846: (Convictions 501) There were 10 males under 17 years of age sentenced to public whippings and 8 males sentenced to solitary confinement. Twenty prisoners sentenced to transportation.

1874 & 1877: (Convictions 470 and 501) Eight and four prisoners respectively were sentenced to 'Penal Servitude', which had been introduced to replace transportation. This consisted of rigorous cellular isolation and complete non-intercourse by day and night, plank bed, a restricted diet, isolated labour and deprivation of all humanising privileges.

CHAPTER 8

The People – Staff

Details of staff members have been found in Census records (C),[50] Prison Inspectors' reports (IR), Quarter Sessions records (QS),[51] Post Office Directories (PO),[52] Kelly's Directories of Cornwall and Devon & Cornwall (K) [52] and newspapers, for example, Bodmin Guardian (BG).[53] The number after the above abbreviations is the year or date of issue. The lists are not comprehensive as the reports are usually several years apart; however, they do allow trends in staff numbers to be seen and, in some cases, details of the careers of individual people during the life-time of the gaol.

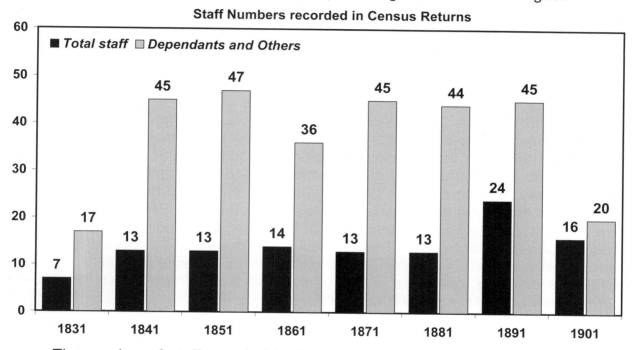

Staff Numbers recorded in Census Returns

The number of staff reported in the decennial census returns range from 7 in 1831 to a high of 24 in 1891. In 1891 and 1901, twelve and seven members of staff were living in the town. In all other cases the staff numbers reported were on the gaol site. The total number of dependants, which included spouses, children, other relatives, servants and visitors, rose from 17 in 1831 to over 40 (range 36 to 47) for other census years before dropping to 20 in 1901. The number of staff and dependants represented 30-44% of the total gaol population, including prisoners, in all census returns except for 1831 and 1901.

The earliest report of staff numbers is contained in an 1815 document: [54] *The governor is allowed a salary of £30 p. a., and if his profits of the prisoners' work (and fees), with the salary do not amount to two hundred pounds, the County pay the deficiency. There are also two Turnkeys, who are paid by the County twelve pounds, with sundry allowances to make up their salaries one hundred pounds per annum each.*

In the 'Inspectors of Prisons' reports for 1843 [12] & 1846 [13], the staff numbers are quoted as 15, this includes the 13 reported posts in the census for 1841 and 1851, and in addition, the surgeon and the clerk, who probably both lived in the town. The corresponding report for 1877[30] lists the governor, chaplain, surgeon, matron and subordinate staff of 16 males and 3 females. This gives a total staff of 23, which is far higher than the census data for 1871 and 1881. The totals for these years do not include staff living off-site. In 1894, the Secretary of State at the Home Office considered that 8 warders, a chief warder and a night watchman was adequate security staff for Bodmin prison.[55] This did not include the Naval Prison or the chaplain, schoolmaster and clerks in the Civil prison.

The main post in the gaol was that of Governor, also known earlier as Keeper of the gaol. The titles Warder-in-Charge (1891) and Chief Warder-in-Charge (1901) were government grades below that of Governor. In an attempt to save money, the government policy, after 1880, was that prisons with less than 101 prisoners on average in the previous year, were not large enough to have the higher grade of governor.[55] There was also a Matron, usually with an assistant, who was responsible for the women prisoners, a Chaplain, who lived on site, and the services of a Surgeon or Medical Officer, daily and as required. During the time of the Naval Prison, a local Catholic Chaplain was available for both civil and naval prisoners. Originally the custodians were called Turnkeys; this was changed between 1847 and 1851, to the title Warder.

Governors (County Gaol and H M Civil Prison)

The first governor of the gaol was Edmund Leach. In January 1780, he complained at the Quarter sessions,[56] that Thomas Jones the contractor, had not completed the buildings in a proper, workmanlike way. The justices dismissed his complaint as groundless and discharged him from office, with immediate effect, because of several instances of misbehaviour. James Chapple, foreman of the builder of the gaol, was appointed temporary gaoler. A post he held for 48 years until his death in 1827. Frederick Chapple, son of James (?) was appointed 'Keeper of the Common Gaol' in October 1827 but at the next Quarter Sessions, John Bentham Everest, a professional gaoler who transferred from the prison hulk at Chatham, was appointed Governor of the House of Correction at Bodmin. There is no further mention of Frederick Chapple and Everest was recorded as governor of the gaol until his retirement in 1860. Effectively there were only two governors of the gaol between 1780 and 1860. This covers approximately 60% of the useful lifetime of the institution.

From Quarter Sessions records it would appear that the two governors were treated quite differently by the ruling Justices. In 1795, the Court noted that the expenses for the gaol were increasing but that no accounts had been received from Chapple since 1781. They ordered accounts to be prepared indicating costs for the subsistence of prisoners, repairs to buildings, expenses in conveying prisoners, fees for discharge, punishment etc., salaries and accounts of prisoner's labour. The Court also called upon Chapple to explain the use of advances made to him to purchase materials for the employment of prisoners. The court had provided £494/9/11¾d for this purpose, of which £218/11/3d had been used for labour on the gaol. Chapple claimed that prisoners might be more usefully employed in the growing and manufacture of flax. He had used some of the advance and his own money to cultivate 34 acres of flax and had made a considerable quantity of course linen called Dowlas. The Court considered that it was improper that the County should engage in such speculative concern. It highly disapproved and ordered that the cultivation and manufacture should be discontinued.

After Everest became governor there is a marked change in the comments of the Court. The Visiting Justices report of April, 1832, noted 'four years have elapsed since total change in system made.' Justices expressed their 'perfect satisfaction'. 'The new governor was appointed 12th February 1828'. Everest organised a major building and repair programme from 1828 so that the gaol conditions conformed to various Acts of Parliament. The Court was so impressed with the running of the gaol, the behaviour of the prisoners and the rebuilding programme that in 1832, it ordered £100 or a piece of plate to that value to be presented to Mr John Bentham Everest in recognition of his valuable service. By 1835, the Justices reported the gaol in excellent order and in a state of progressive improvement. The inspector of Prisons[22], wrote the following tribute to governor Everest after his retirement:

> "Advancing age and infirmity have deprived the County of the services of an officer who has long and deservedly enjoyed the reputation of being one of the best of prison governors. M. Everest has in that capacity had to struggle with the all but insurmountable obstacles presented by an ill-constructed prison, which, besides other disadvantages was far too small for the convenient confinement of its inmates, and it is not too much to say that his talent, energy, and activity so completely triumphed over these difficulties as to render the County prison of Cornwall one of the best conducted establishments of the kind in the kingdom, and to reduce the expenses quite as much as, the discipline was improved."

List of Governors. County Gaol and Civil Prison			
	From	To	Recorded in:
Edmund Leach	1779?	1780	QS1780
James Chapple	1780	1827	QS1827
Frederick Chapple	1827		QS1827
John Bentham Everest	Jan.1828	1860	QS1828, C1831, C1851
Hugh George Colvill	ca.1860	post 1873	C1861, C1871, PO1873
Maj. E W Lane	pre 1881	1883	C1881
Vacancy	1883		K1883
Mr Parr	1883		Nat.Arch. T 1/15534
William Stevens	ca. 1883	1896	K1889, C1891, K1893
Wm. Repulsa Shenton	1896	post 1901	K1897, C1901
Henry Leonard Browett	pre 1906	1916	K1906, K1914

The Governors after Everest, were Hugh George Colvill, Major E W Lane, there was a vacancy in 1883 then Mr Parr, William Stevens, followed by William Repulsa Shenton and finally Henry Leonard Browett (See page 38) until the civil prison closed.

Governors (H. M. Naval Prison)

After 1887, when the Naval Prison was established, there were separate governors for this part of the prison. The official job title seems to have been Deputy Governor of H M Prison or H M Naval prison. The first governor was Commander Malcolm McNeile, followed by Captain G S McIlwaine, for three months and M B Cartwright for less than a year. Commander Pearson Campbell Johnstone served until ca.1910 and the final governor, Commander Thomas Brandreth remained until the closure of the Naval Prison.

List of Governors. Naval Prison			
	From	To	Recorded in:
Comm. Malcolm McNeile	1887	1890	K1889
Captain G S McIlwaine	1890	1890	BG 7/1/1922, p4
M B Cartwright	1890	1890/1	BG 7/1/1922, p4
Comm. Pearson Campbell Johnstone	1891	1910	C1891, K1893, K1906
Comm. Thomas Brandreth	1910	1922	K1914

It is believed that the 'Naval Governor' lived in one of two gaol villas built in 1892 but documents show that the holder of this position never lived on the gaol site. Commander McNeile had a very famous son, Lt. Col. Herman Cyril McNeile, who under the pen-name 'Sapper', wrote books featuring *'Bulldog Drummond'*. As a character, Drummond has been compared with Sherlock Holmes, Raffles and the Saint. The character finally disappeared in the 1950s with the introduction of James Bond. There are many published reports that 'Sapper' was born in the Naval Prison on 28th September, 1888. In fact, his birth certificate states that he was born at his father's residence in Higher Bore Street. A few months later *(K1889)* the address is recorded as St. Leonard's, Lower Bore Street, Bodmin. Of the other governors, for which we have details, Commander P C Johnstone lived in Windsor Cottage, Castle Street and Thomas Brandreth lived in 'Rockleigh', St. Nicholas Street, Bodmin.

Chaplains (County Gaol and H M Civil Prison)

In 1802, the appointment of Rev. Moses Morgan as chaplain to the County Gaol was revoked. The Court ordered that he be appointed chaplain to the gaol and bridewell at Bodmin at the yearly salary of £50. He died in 1810 and was replaced by George Thomas Plummer, who resigned in 1812. Joseph Fayrer, appointed 1812, was chaplain until 1822 when he was replaced by Leonard Jarvis Boor, who held the position until his death in 1835. In 1823 the salary had increased to £150 p a. After the death of Boor, the services were taken alternately by Nicholas and Francis John Hext Kendall. Francis Kendall held the post from 1836 to 1845 when he was replaced by his brother, Nicholas. In 1847, the salary was £200 p a. William Frederick Everest was chaplain from before 1861 to after 1883 and he was followed by Charles Boutflower Simpson (pre1891 to post 1901). Samuel Percy Hammond Statham and Thomas Austin held the position in 1906 and 1914 respectively.

List of Chaplains. County Gaol, Civil & Naval Prisons			
	From	**To**	**Recorded in:**
John Lethbridge		1797	QS1797
Moses Morgan	1797	1810	QS1802
George Thomas Plummer	July 1810	Apr 1812	QS1810, QS1812
Joseph Fayrer	July1812	1822	QS1812
Leonard Jarvis Boor	1822	1835	QS1823, QS1835
Nicholas Kendall Francis John Hext Kendall	1835	1836	QS1835
Francis J H Kendall	10/1835	1845	QS1836, IR1844
Nicholas Kendall	1845	?	IR1847
William Frederick Everest	pre 1861	post 1883	C1861, C1881, K1883
Charles Boutflower Simpson	pre 1891	post 1901	C1891, K1897, C1901
Samuel Percy Statham	post 1901	pre 1914	K1906
Thomas Austin	pre 1914	?	K1914

Kelly's Directories contain the following names as Catholic chaplains: Felix Menchini (1889), Augustine H White (1893), Cuthbert McAdam (1897), Aloysius Smith (1906) and Alphonsus McElroy (1914).

Matrons (County Gaol and H M Civil Prison)

Before ca.1900, all the Matrons & Assistant Matrons were related to other members of the gaol staff. Jane Peter was married to the gaol clerk William Peter,

Elizabeth White was the wife of Thomas White, warder, and Mary H Stevens was the governor's wife. Holders of these positions are listed in the following Table:

Date	Matron	Assistant Matron	Date	Matron	Assistant Matron
1831	Mary Ann Dungey		1871	Ann Dungey	Jane Peter Mary Dungey
1841	Mary Ann Dungey	Ann Dungey	1881	Mary Dungey	
1851	Ann Dungey	Jane Peter	1891	Mary H Stevens	
1861	Ann Dungey	Jane Peter Edna Ann Dungey Elizabeth White	1902	Lucy Curnick	
			1906	Adelaide Marshall	

The situation with the Dungey family is more complicated. A partial family tree shows the relationships in the family. Thomas (born ca.1770) was appointed turnkey in 1790, his son Thomas (born 1791), joined the staff in 1819, was promoted to Head Turnkey in 1828 and Principal turnkey in 1841. His sister(?) Mary Ann was matron in 1831 & 1841 and his wife Ann, assistant matron from 1840 and matron in 1851, 1861 & 1871. Their daughter, Edna Ann, was assistant matron in 1861 and their other daughter, Mary, was matron in 1881. Members of this family were employed in the gaol from 1790 to post 1881. This covers over 91 years of the gaol's 127 year history.

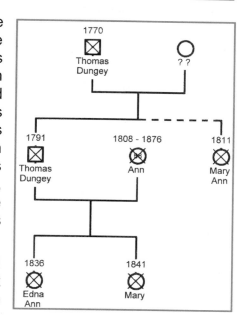

In the later years, when the gaol was H M Prison, Bodmin, the staff were civil servants and it seems likely that the members of staff were rotated to other prisons on a regular basis.

Surgeons & Medical Officers (County Gaol, Civil & Naval Prisons)

William Hamley was the surgeon to the gaol from before 1797 to 1810. From 1797 to 1803, Peter Edward Scobell was joint surgeon with Hamley. Joseph Hamley was appointed surgeon, in place of his father, in 1810. He remained in the post until after 1847. In 1810, his salary was £30 p.a.; it was gradually increased and reached £90 p.a. in 1847. Thomas Quiller-Couch, father of Sir Arthur Quiller-Couch, was surgeon in 1883. Bartholomew Gidley Derry was Medical Officer from the 1880s until after 1914.

List of Surgeons. County Gaol, Civil & Naval Prisons			
	From	**To**	**Recorded in:**
William Hamley	pre 1797	1810	QS 1797, QS 1810
Peter Edward Scobell (joint)	1797	1803	QS 1797, QS 1803
Joseph Hamley	1810	post 1847	QS 1810, QS 1823,
Thomas Quiller Couch			K1883
Bartholomew Gidley Derry	pre 1889	post 1914	K1889, K1906, K1914

List of Staff Employed in Bodmin Gaol

A list of people employed in the gaol (Appendix 3) contains over 100 names, including the governors, chaplains, matrons and surgeons mentioned above. The County Gaol was a place of stable employment; there are several examples of people working there for over 20 years. Included in this group are the governors Chapple and Everest, the turnkey/messenger, Philip Corney (49 years). The turnkeys, Thomas Dungey (>32 years), James Holman (>43 years), John Martin (>30 years) and William Osbourn (>21 years), the surgeons Joseph Hamley and B G Derry, the matrons, Jane Peter and Ann Dungey and Chaplain William Frederick Everest. The officer Richard Doidge received a long service medal, possibly for 25 years service.

Family members were also employed, in addition to the Dungey family, there are four examples of fathers and sons both working in the gaol. They are Hamley, Hill, Martin and White. There are two people each called Holman, Sowden, James and Richard. No relationship between them has been found. There are entries for William Anguin and William Angwin, it seems likely that the first spelling is an error.

Some records give job descriptions in place of just 'Warder' or 'Turnkey'. William Hill is described as Superintendent of Treadwheel, Thomas White as shoemaker/turnkey and James Tucker & Thomas Davey, as Miller/Warder. The position of gaol engineer was held by William Angwin (1861 & 1871) and by Joseph Worth in 1881. In the same year, Charles Jane was Cook/Baker and Albert J Titford had the title Warder/Cook in 1891. Clerk of the gaol was William Peter, from 1843 until after 1851, William Anguin (or Angwin) in 1873 and Joseph Baker from before 1883 to after 1897. In 1902, William Hurch was Clerk/Storekeeper. Edwin Albert Extence (1906) and Samuel Edmund Chapman (1914) held the post of Clerk/Schoolmaster.

In the Naval prison, John James was Clerk/Storekeeper, followed by Joseph Edmunds and Samuel George Luscombe (1906). In 1902, Edmunds became Chief Warder of the Naval Prison.

The sale document of 1929 labelled the two villas on either side of the main Naval Prison gate as Chief and Principal Officer's Quarters but they were the only accommodation for naval staff on the site. As previously stated, the Naval governors lived in houses in the town. In 1891 & 1901, the chief warder, Warren S Gearing, and the warder, Thomas H Lockyer, lived in the gaol. All other members of staff lived in the town. The warder George H Sandford lived in Stanley Terrace. The schoolmaster, Osborne Walker, and the warder, William Thomas White, both lived in Cribbage Terrace. The clerks, James, Edmunds and Luscombe lived in Morton Villa, Gaol Lane; Chelston Cottage and 'Fernside', St Nicholas Street.

Dudley Prout Collection

CHAPTER 9

The People – Inmates

There are a number of documents, including census returns, Inspectors reports, a few Governors' reports and the reports of Howard (1779 & 1787)[2,3] and Neild (1803)[57], which give the numbers of prisoners in the gaol. This is a very small sample of the population as the reports account for the number of prisoners on 28 days in the ca.140 years of the gaol history.

There are some problems with even this small amount of data. In the 39th report of the Inspectors of Prisons (1875), which records a total of 84 prisoners for 29th September, 1874, it states *'that the number of civil prisoners having been unusually small of late, empty cells have been used to house naval and military personnel'*. From November 1873 to the report date, 227 naval prisoners committed under the *'Naval Discipline Act'*, had been transferred to Bodmin from H M ships at Devonport. The number of naval & military prisoners present on the date of the visit is not included in the report.

Total Number of Inmates in the County Gaol & H. M. Civil Prison, Bodmin. Each Recorded on a Single Day in the Year.

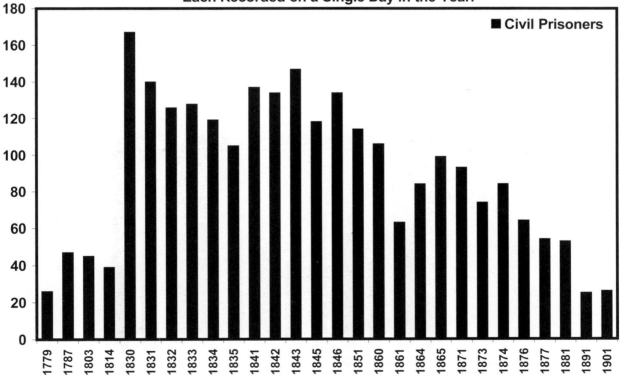

The 1881 census clearly marks naval/military prisoners by indicating the regiment or Royal Navy, in the return. After the transfer of the two buildings to the Admiralty, the practice of keeping naval prisoners in the civil wing continued. There were two types of naval prisoners in the gaol. Prisoners whose sentence included 'dismissal from the service' had to be housed in a Civil Prison, rather than a Naval Prison. The 1891 census again identifies naval/army prisoners in the civil block but the 1901 enumerator assumed that only civil prisoners were housed in the civil gaol. This error was partially corrected by the census supervisor. He marked 13 marines in the civil section as 'Navymen' but failed to notice 11 stokers, 21 seamen and a R N clerk. In the previous returns these 'job titles' applied to naval prisoners and, in addition, very few merchant seamen were recorded in earlier documents. For convenience, these ex-navymen are included in the Naval Prison population, to distinguish them from civil prisoners.

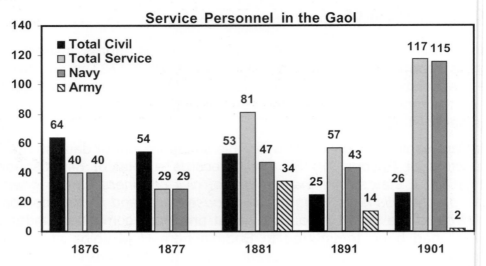

This chart shows the total service prisoners in the gaol and compares the numbers with the total civil prisoners for years between 1876 and 1901. In 1881, 1891 & 1901, the number of Naval & Army prisoners outnumbered the civil prisoners. The number of prisoners was higher in 1881, before the Naval Prison was established, than in 1891 and it increased in 1901 to over twice the 1891 level. Army prisoners decreased from 34 in 1881 to 14 in 1891 and only 2 in 1901.

The above data consists of 'one off' counts of prisoners and do not give an accurate picture of the total number of prisoners that went through the gaol. For some years data is available for the total number of committals.

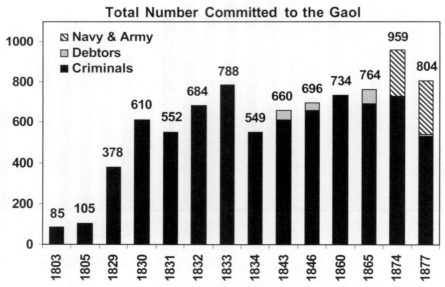

The above data is not complete, for example, some reports only contain numbers for prisoners, which may or may not include debtors and Army & Navy personnel. Some of the numbers are explained in Governor's and Chaplain's reports. In 1829, the Chaplain stated that there was a greater proportion of juvenile offenders *"chiefly for robbing orchards and gardens"*.[58] The Governor stated, in October, 1832, *"that 90 vagrants were committed since his last quarterly report, being exactly half the total of all prisoners."* The vagrant problem was largely moved from the gaol to the work-house after 1842.[59]

In addition to the data in the chart, there are other sets of numbers. Howard reports that between 13th January 1780 and 27th July 1782, there were 261 committals, consisting of 75 debtors, 92 felons, etc. and 94 petty offenders. L. E. Long in *'An Old Cornish Town'* [25] states that during the first 27 years of its existence, 3,877 prisoners passed through the gaol, of whom 1,258 were criminals, 773 were debtors and the remaining 1,846 had been confined in the Bridewell.

Description of Gaol Population by Sex and Age

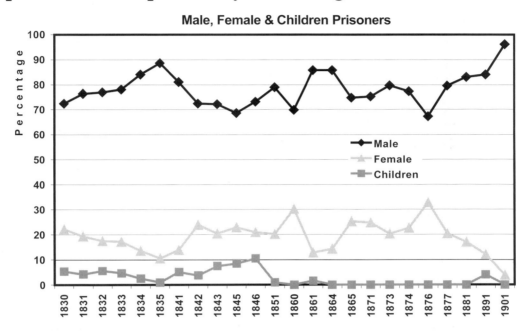

Male, Female & Children Prisoners

For most of the lifetime of the gaol, the ratio of male to female prisoners averaged 4:1. After 1876, the number of female prisoners started to decrease, until in 1901, there was only one female prisoner. The number of children prisoners after about 1850 was generally nil, except for two 12 year olds, one in 1861 and the other in 1891. There were cases of infants with their mothers but these are not included. These numbers for children seem to be lower than the national averages. Although after the Reformatory School Act of 1864, imprisonment of children was reduced, it was not until the Children Act of 1908, that it was abolished.

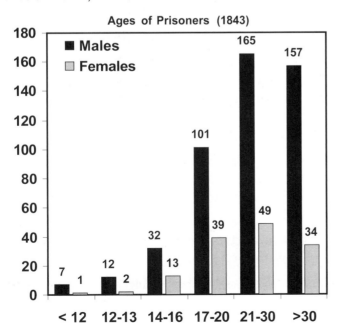

Ages of Prisoners (1843)

For the year 1843, the total committals, including those for trial, was 474 male and 138 female prisoners. There were 67 prisoners below the age of seventeen, 51 boys and 16 girls. Nineteen boys and three girls were below the age of thirteen.

Approximately 60% of the prisoners were in the 17 to 29 age group.

Description of Gaol Population by Type of Prisoner

The population of the gaol did not just consist of convicted prisoners; some were waiting to go to trial while others, like debtors, were not even criminals. The prisoners were also felons or misdemeanants, that is, serious or minor offenders.

For the years 1830 to 1834, the governor John Bentham Everest, prepared a series of reports for the Quarter Sessions.[60] The reports contain numbers for each of the different types of prisoner. The average numbers for each group, over the five years and the percentage of the gaol population are shown in the following table:

Prisoner Type	Male		Female	
	Number	%	Number	%
Convicted Misdemeanour	45.4	35.0	13.0	10.0
Convicted Felony	24.2	18.7	3.6	2.8
Charged Felony	17.6	13.6	4.4	3.4
Debtors	12.8	9.8	0.8	0.6
Charged Misdemeanour	6.8	5.2	1.0	0.8

The groups are debtors, male and female representing 9.8% and 0.6% of the total prisoners; convicted of felony (18.7 & 2.8%) and charged with felony (13.6 & 3.4%). The largest group, convicted of misdemeanours and imprisoned for want of sureties (35 & 10%) and the smallest group, charged with misdemeanours (5.2 & 0.8%).

The Reports of the Inspectors of Prisons, published in 1844[12] and 1847/8,[13] contained a full account of the gaol population and their disposal for the years ending September 1843 and September 1846.

In September, 1842, at the start of the year covered, there were 41 prisoners for trial. During the year, there were 223 new prisoners for trial and 63 rendered (brought) to Court, giving a total of 327 to be tried. Of the 327 cases for trial, 219 went to the quarter sessions, 160 (113 male + 47 female) for felonies and 59 (52 + 7) for misdemeanours and 108 to the assizes, 96 (72 + 24) for felonies and 12 (8 + 4) for misdemeanours.

What happened to these people? 148 were sentenced to Bodmin Gaol, 31 were transported, 5 were whipped, fined or discharged on sureties, 68 were acquitted at the Bar, 37 no Bills found (the Bill of Indictment was a written accusation, which had to be presented to the Court before a Trial), 9 were not prosecuted and 29 left for trial at the end of the year.

In addition, there were 326 prisoners under Summary Convictions. They included 47 at the start of the year; the remaining 279 were imprisoned for the following reasons: By Courts Martial (10); Deserter (1); Under the Game Laws (4); Revenue Laws (5); Vagrant Act (132); Malicious Trespass Act (25); Larceny Act (25); Assault (58); Want of Sureties (10) and other Summary Convictions (56).

There were 13 debtors at the start of the year and this increased to 48 (45 male & 3 female) during the year September 1842 to September 1843.

The corresponding data for the year ending September 1846 is contained in Appendix 4.

Later in the century, debtors were not imprisoned and the distinction between felons and misdemeanants was removed. This gave a classification system of prisoners which contained only two groups, those charged with a crime and those sentenced by the courts.

Length of Sentence

Terms of Imprisonment for Convicted Prisoners														
Sentence	1812		1822		1832		1843		1846		1874		1877	
	M	F	M	F	M	F	M	F	M	F	M	F	M	F
7 days or less	1		5	2	5						67	30	51	34
14 days or less							8	1	4	4				
> 7 days to 14 days		1	3	2	7	4					39	35	88	36
> 14 days to 1 month	1	1	8	1	20	2	47	10	29	16	109	36	112	34
> 1 m to 3 months	7	1	8	2	18	4	198	55	187	81	97	14	87	25
> 3 m to 6 months			8	2	17	6	68	20	80	18	22	8	20	4
> 6 m to 1 year			2		16	2	37	9	39	9	10		8	
> 1 y to 2 years	1				2		15	5	10	2	3		1	1
> 2 y to 3 years							1		1	1				
Total	10	3	34	9	85	18	374	100	350	131	347	123	367	134

This table contains the numbers of prisoners sentenced to different lengths of imprisonment for seven selected years between 1812 and 1877.

Bodmin Gaol was a local prison and generally only accepted prisoners serving two years or less. In addition, it housed prisoners before trial, prisoners sentenced to transportation and those to be hanged. Prisoners sentenced to periods of imprisonment over two years would be sent to a Convict prison, for example, Dartmoor.

Changes in the Gaol Population

The increase in the population of the gaol, before the 1830s, mirrors the population increase in the county.[61] There are two possible reasons for this. Firstly, this was a time of massive growth in the mining industry and, secondly, at the end of the Napoleonic wars in 1815, many unemployed soldiers and sailors returned, searching for work and this led to an increase in crime.

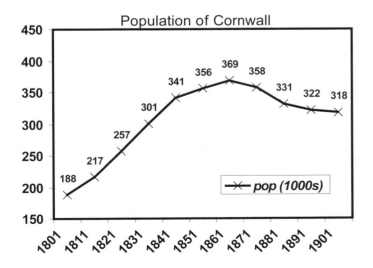

The peak in 1830 was caused by the closure of the County Gaol at Launceston. After this there was a slow steady decrease during the remainder of the 19th century. The population statistics do not explain the fall in prisoner numbers after about 1841 as the total population of the county was still increasing at this time.

Reasons for the decrease in the gaol population could include new Acts of Parliament, for example, the Debtor's Act of 1869, which virtually ended imprisonment for debt and later in the century, the practice of issuing 'fines' rather than sending guilty people to prison.

However, in the third quarter of the nineteenth century, when the prison population was in decline, the number of committals to the gaol remained high.

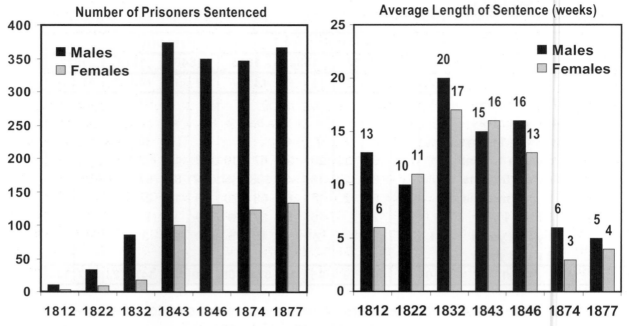

In the years 1843, 1846, 1874 & 1877, the number of prisoners sentenced to Bodmin Gaol remained constant but over the same years, the number of prisoners in the gaol decreased from 147 to 54.

The explanation for this lies in the length of sentences handed down by the magistrates and judges. The 1812 data is from a very small sample and the average sentences for that year are probably not reliable. There was an increase between 1822 and 1832 and a slight drop in the 1840s. Between the 1840s and the 1870s, the average sentence length decreased from about 15 weeks to only 3-6 weeks.

In summary, the increase in the gaol population in the early eighteen century was caused by a large increase in the County population. The decrease in prisoner numbers, after about 1870 was not due to less crime but to a significant reduction in the length of sentences handed down by the judges and magistrates. By about the mid 1870s there was no need for a prison of this size in Cornwall.

BUTTONS

Cornwall County   H M Prisons   Naval Prison
Gaol (pre 1875)   (post 1875)   Bodmin

CHAPTER 10

Gaol - Rules and Punishments

"The distress of prisoners, of which there are few who have not some imperfect idea, came more immediately under my notice when I was sheriff of the county of Bedford; and the circumstance which excited me to activity in their behalf was, the seeing, some—who by the verdict of juries were declared not guilty; some—on whom the grand jury did not find such an appearance of guilt as subjected them to trial; and some—whose prosecutors did not appear against them;—after having been confined for months, dragged back to gaol, and locked up again till they should pay sundry fees to the gaoler, the clerk of assize, etc." This quote from Howard describes the unjust treatment of prisoners who were found not guilty of the crime. They were kept, like those who had been convicted; some in dungeons, without regular food or a supply of water, in airless dark quarters, windows were blocked up due to the window tax, payable by the gaoler. All types of prisoners, debtors, felons and bridewell, were together and they had to pay charges to the gaoler, turnkeys and court clerks and for all services, including beds, straw, fees chargeable on arrival (garnish) and discharge and even fees for punishments, such as whipping and 'being put in irons'. It was legal at the time for prisoners to earn money by working, however, in many gaols there were no tools or suitable work spaces.

How different were the conditions in the new Bodmin Gaol in the late 18th Century? A prisoner arriving at Bodmin would see a set of prison buildings, unlike any seen before - buildings which would not be out of place in some of our famous Georgian cities. He would never have seen a gaol which had individual cells, baths, running water, an infirmary and chapel. Life would still be hard, charges had not been abolished but he would have opportunities to earn money to pay them. He would be forced to work hard, the food would be limited, as the cost of the food had to be below that spent by local poor families, he would have to be silent at all times, even when working with others and to attend chapel. On the other hand, he would be kept healthy, the services of the surgeon were not available to most of the population, and he would probably be in better condition on leaving the gaol than on arrival. This is a great difference to earlier institutions, where the chances of dying of gaol fever, smallpox or malnutrition were very high.

There is a contemporary document by Howard, published in the third edition of his book *'The State of Prisons'*. This covered his journey of Great Britain and Ireland in 1782. In this edition, there is a report on the new County Gaol at Bodmin. In addition to a description of the facilities, it lists a table of fees and rates to be taken by the gaoler and turnkeys and a set of Articles, Regulations and Allowances. These documents define the conditions and the daily life of the prisoners in the gaol.

County Gaol at Bodmin (1782)

'This new gaol is built on a fine eminence, at a little distance from the town, where there is a constant current of water. Here is a good house for the gaoler, in which there are apartments for master's-side debtors, and a chapel. There are separate rooms and courts for each sex of debtors, of felons, and of petty offenders or bridewell prisoners; and each prisoner has a separate lodging-room (about eight feet two inches by five feet eight, and seven and a half feet high), which is furnished with a bedstead, straw-bed, two blankets and a coverlet. There are two rooms for an infirmary, and under them three condemned cells. In two of the courts are baths. In the centre of the gaoler's house there

is a turret with an alarm-bell and clock. The men who are confined for petty offences, are employed in sawing and polishing stone, and, as they have the county allowance (food and necessities paid for by the county), keep only one-sixth of what they earn. Clauses against spirituous liquors are hung up. The Act for preserving the health of prisoners is not hung up, but the gaol is now kept very neat and clean.

A table of fees and regulations were printed and hung up, though not signed. The majority of the fees and rates applied to debtors. The only charge for felons and persons committed to the bridewell was a discharge or acquittal fee of 13s.4d'.

The Rules and Regulations (1782) defined the conditions and the daily life and diet of the prisoners. All prisoners were employed for 10 hr. per day in the summer and 8 hr. in winter. The keeper kept one sixth of their earnings, the prisoner one sixth plus the full amount for extra work, the rest went to the county toward the expense of their maintenance. The working day started with a bell rung at sunrise, from the 1st November to 31st March, and at 6 a.m. for the rest of the year. Locking-up time was 6 p.m. from 1st October - 31st March and 8 p.m. during the remainder of the year.

The list of offences against prison rules included:- Abuse, ill-treatment or affray between prisoners; playing games for money or liquor; entering a cell during the day, except for cleaning; bad behaviour and failing to attend divine service. These offences were punishable by close confinement, harder labour or reduction in diet. Irons were provided, at the county expense, and kept ready to be used, when absolutely necessary for punishment.

The head gaoler kept a register containing the following details of each prisoner: - Date of confinement - Person's name - Place of abode - By whom confined - For what offence - Stature, complexion, etc. - Where discharged or how disposed of – Remarks on behaviour, etc. The justices of Bodmin sessions, the grand jury at the assizes and all justices of the peace and the sheriff and his deputy, were all requested to visit the gaol and bridewell, as often as possible, to inquire into the state and treatment of all prisoners and debtors.

The situation of debtors in prison was complex. They were imprisoned by their creditors, who were expected to support them. Master or principle debtors of property could choose their room in the keeper's house and their bed and diet at the rates fixed by the keeper. Ordinary debtors were housed over the arcades according to their choice or ability to pay the established rates. Debtors were allowed to work and to keep all of their earnings.

The design of the new gaol, together with reasonable charges and defined regulations and allowances demonstrate that Bodmin was the first modern prison built in Britain. At the same time in Launceston, the prisoners were still in a dungeon and were fed through a hole in the ceiling!

After the death of Howard in 1790, the work of inspecting prisons was taken over by James Neild. In his report, after his visit in 1803,[57] he repeats many of the comments made by Howard but there are differences. He states that the prisoners keep one-half of their earnings, rather than one-sixth and that they work in a large work-room, in which there are several looms for weaving and a court, 46 yards by 32 yards, to work in. All the apartments were whitewashed twice a year and the sleeping cells, four times. The floors of the dayrooms and sleeping-cells were washed once a week in winter, and twice in summer, and swept every day. He had two complaints about the gaol, firstly, there was association between committed prisoners and those sentenced and, secondly, there was no separation of *young beginners* from *old offenders*.

Some interesting references to the gaol and bridewell are contained in a report printed by order of the Honourable Court of Aldermen of the City of London, on September 26th, 1815.[54] The report was drawn up by a committee which set out from London on July 29th, 1814, to visit the gaol of Gloucester, and such other gaols as they deemed expedient, so that they might become acquainted with their main features and compare them with those of some of the gaols in the City of London.

Describing the prison at Bodmin, the report of 1815 says that it *was built upwards of thirty years ago. It stands on the side of a hill near the town of Bodmin, so that the buildings range one above another; and every part is well supplied with excellent water distributed throughout for the supply of baths and for other purposes.*

The Governor's house is in the centre of the Prison, as is also the Chapel, the seats of which are so placed, that the men are kept distinct from the women, and entirely out of sight of each other, and the Debtors as placed in the Gallery.

This Prison will contain thirty-six men, besides women, and thirty Debtors. There were at the time of the Committee's Visit nineteen men in the Gaol, and sixteen men and four women in the Bridewell, and the average number in the two Prisons is stated to be forty-two.

The criminals are generally placed two in a cell, and are sometimes, ironed, and no preference whatever is allowed to be given to any prisoner by paying for it. Innocent exercises, conducive to health, are allowed; but all sorts of games for money or liquor are entirely prohibited. The prisoners are all employed in some work, and those committed to hard labour are strictly kept thereto. One-sixth part of their earnings is given to the Governor, one-sixth to themselves, and the remainder is paid into the County-stock towards the expenses of their maintenance.

The Debtors are allowed to work, and have all their earnings; and visitors are admitted generally to them during the day. The Allowance of Bread to the Debtors is the same as to the other prisoners; but they are restricted to the purchase of one quart of beer or cyder each day.

This report seems to confirm that the cell numbers are the same as those identified on the John Call engraving and that the comment on the bottom of the document, *'One Hundred Men and Women may be lodged in the several Wards at the same time'* could not be achieved without placing two prisoners in each cell.

In accordance with the Prison Act of 1823,[62] the Justices published a new set of Rules & Regulations in October, 1823. The rules included: the keeper must have no financial interest in prison supplies or sell anything to prisoners; he must inspect every cell and see every prisoner daily; he must record all punishments and other 'occurrences of importance'. The chaplain to read selected prayers every morning and all convicted prisoners to attend divine service. Prisoners not to be put in irons, except when absolutely necessary.

New sets of 'Prison Rules & Regulations' were produced at various times throughout the history of the gaol. The Rules, introduced in July, 1832[63] and a later set, undated but probably late Victorian are reproduced below. The breaking of any of these Rules resulted in punishment.

Rules and regulations for treatment of prisoners in Bodmin Gaol and House of Correction at Bodmin (July 1832).

1. On arrival all prisoners to be cleansed and examined. Money, watches, knives and articles likely to be of use in escape attempts to be taken from them and listed by principal turnkey in a book kept for that purpose, all to be restored to owners on discharge.
2. Prisoners with no money, whose behaviour has been good, to be allowed a small sum on discharge, at discretion of governor.
3. Convicted prisoners not to receive any food, clothing or "necessaries" other than gaol allowance.
4. Established diet to be maintained. No wines, spirits or beer to be allowed except by direction of visiting justices, or by surgeon in case of prisoner's sickness.
5. Prisoners on remand to be allowed food, clothing and necessaries subject to examination.
6. Prisoners sentenced to hard labour and employed on hand mill, treadwheel or other work to be allowed up to extra ½lb of bread.
7. Prisoners not sentenced to hard labour to be set to work "not severe" and if able to earn their own subsistence. If more than subsistence amount earned by a prisoner, the surplus money to be paid on prisoner's discharge, subject to good conduct.
8. Prisoners on remand to be allowed to work for remuneration with their own consent.
9. All letters written by, or sent to prisoners to be read by Governor or principal turnkey but prisoners on remand not subject to this rule, and to be allowed pens, ink and paper.
10. Prisoners on remand to be allowed to see their friends and legal advisers.
11. Turnkeys forbidden to strike prisoners or to use abusive language. Cases of misconduct to be reported to governor.

Rules to be observed by prisoners

1. To be respectful to prison officers, and to obey turnkeys' orders. To be clean and "peaceable and orderly".
2. No gaming, fighting or wrestling, or abusive language.
3. No money to be extracted from fellow prisoners, nor to ill treat them.
4. To observe strict silence whilst working or locked in sleeping cells. No shouting or unnecessary noise at other times.
5. No clothes to be destroyed. No damage to county property.
6. No water to be boiled "in your Tin pots" and no cooking in dayrooms. No smoking or use of tobacco.
7. Wards-men to be responsible for clean state of their ward and good order.

Rules for prisoners confined for debt in Sheriff's Ward.

1. Debtors not to be subjected to any more regulations other than that necessary for their safe custody, and the discipline and hygiene of the prison.
2. Debtors paying their own expenses may occupy the best apartments, but those not paying to be allocated other accommodation.
3. Debtors' bedrooms to be opened at the same time as those of other prisoners and occupants to vacate their bedrooms by 9 a.m. unless prevented by sickness, and be locked up at 10p.m. at lights out.
4. Each debtor to make his/her bed, and clean the room by 11 a.m., and wash it at least once a week. Bedding to be aired. If more than one debtor in a bedroom to take turns with cleaning. Dayrooms to be cleaned daily.
5. No food to be prepared in bedrooms. Food to be cooked to be "dressed" in dayroom or at the lodge by permission of the turnkey.
6. No tobacco to be smoked in bedrooms or galleries. No tippling in the ward.
7. Debtors may receive from their friends, or purchase, a pint of wine or a quart of strong beer or cider daily, to be received between 8 a.m. and 1 p.m. Any attempt to obtain more liquor to lose the privilege of his allowance.
8. Debtors, "destitute of friends" or unable to support themselves, may receive the county allowance on production of a certificate from the parish to which they belong, stating their need. Debtors receiving their 6d. or allowance from their creditors not entitled to allowance until their means exhausted.
9. All clothing, liquor, bundles and parcels brought into prison liable to inspection by governor or turnkeys.
10. Debtors permitted to follow their professions, providing their own tools, may keep any earnings therefrom; "except dissenters".
11. All debtors to attend divine service in gaol chapel on Sundays and when held on other days. Those who refuse to be locked in their bedrooms during the service and to be deprived of their liquor allowance next day.
12. No gaming. Any cards or dice found will be destroyed.
13. Debtors to keep themselves clean. Those maintained by county to be allowed soap and towels and their linen to be washed in the prison wash kitchen.
14. Debtors' friends may visit them on any day except Sunday, Christmas day and Good Friday, between 10 a.m. and sunset. No visitor except a wife, husband, parent or child to stay more than an hour or be admitted more than twice a day. No visitors allowed in galleries, bedrooms, or even day rooms when a visiting room provided.
15. Visitors refusing to leave, or misbehaving in any way to be refused admission in future.
16. Disobedience to the rules subject to punishment or privation determined by visiting justices.
17. Female debtors to be kept in a separate ward under control of the matron, and subject to foregoing rules.

ABSTRACT OF THE REGULATIONS
RELATING TO THE
TREATMENT AND CONDUCT
OF
CONVICTED PRISONERS

1. Prisoners shall preserve silence.
2. They shall not communicate, or attempt to do so, with one another, or with any strangers or others who may visit the Prison.
3. They shall keep themselves clean and decent in their persons and shall obey such regulations as regards washing, bathing, and in the case of male prisoners, hair-cutting, as may from time to time be established, with a view to the proper maintenance of health and cleanliness.
4. They shall keep their cells, utensils, clothing, and bedding, clean and neatly arranged; and shall, when required, clean and sweep the yards, passages, and other parts of the prison.
5. If any prisoner has any complaint to make regarding the diet, it must be made immediately after a meal is served. Frivolous and groundless complaints, repeatedly made, will be dealt with a breach of Prison discipline.
6. A prisoner may if required for purposes of justice, be photographed and measured on reception and subsequently.
7. A prisoner committed to Prison for non-payment of a sum adjudged to be paid by the conviction of any court of summary jurisdiction, may obtain a reduction of a part of the sentence by paying part of the sum for which he is liable, viz., the fine, costs, and cost of commitment. No such payment shall be made on Sunday, or on a week-day before 9a .m.
8. Prisoners shall attend Divine Service on Sundays and on other days when such Service is performed, unless they receive permission to be absent. Prisoners shall not be compelled to attend the religious service of a Church to which they do not belong.
9. If any Prisoner who is of a religious persuasion different from that of the Established Church specially so requests, the Governor shall permit a minister of that persuasion to visit him at proper and reasonable times under regulations approved by the Commissioners.
10. The following offences committed by prisoners will render them liable to punishment:—
    1. Disobeying any order of the Governor or of any other officer, or any Prison regulation.
    2. Treating with disrespect any officer or servant of the Prison, or any visitor, or any person employed in connection with the Prison or works.
    3. Being idle, careless, or negligent at work, or refusing to work.
    4. Being absent without leave from Divine Service, or prayers, or school instruction.
    5. Behaving irreverently at Divine Service of prayers.
    6. Swearing, cursing, or using any abusive, insolent, threatening, or other improper language.
    7. Being indecent in language, act, or gesture.
    8. Committing a common assault upon another prisoner.
    9. Conversing or holding intercourse with another prisoner without authority.
    10. Singing, whistling, or making any unnecessary noise, or giving any unnecessary trouble.
    11. Leaving his cell or other appointed location, or his place or work, without permission.
    12. In any way disfiguring or damaging any part of the Prison, or any article to which he may have access.
    13. Committing any nuisance.
    14. Having in his cell or possession any article he is not allowed to have.
    15. Giving to or receiving from any prisoner any article whatever without leave.
    16. In any other way offending against good order and discipline.
    17. Attempting to do any of the foregoing things.
    18. Personal violence to a fellow prisoner.
    19. Grossly offensive or abusive language to any officer or servant of the Prison.
    20. Wilfully or wantonly breaking the Prison windows, or otherwise destroying the Prison property.
    21. When under punishment, wilfully making a disturbance tending to interrupt the order and discipline of the Prison.
    22. Any other act of gross misconduct or insubordination requiring to be suppressed by extraordinary means.
    23. Escaping or attempting to escape from Prison.
11. The following offences committed by male prisoners will render them liable to corporal punishment:—
    1. Mutiny or incitement to mutiny.
    2. Gross personal violence to any officer or servant of the Prison.
12. Prisoners may, if they desire, have an interview with the Governor or Superior Authority, to make complaints or prefer requests; and the Governor shall redress any grievance or take such steps as may seem necessary.

13. Any prisoner wishing to see a member of the Visiting Committee shall be allowed to do so on the occasion of his next occurring visit to the Prison.

Punishments for Prison Offences.

The following table is a compilation of the numbers of prison punishments for breaking the Rules and Regulations:

The Numbers of Punishments for Prison Offences

Year	1830	1831	1832	1833	1843		1846		1865		1870		1874		1877	
					M	F	M	F	M	F	M	F	M	F	M	F
Prisoners	610	552	684	788	474	138	495	166	690		(600)		600	132	390	139
Solitary confinement	115	31	44	14	32	11					10	18	}20		12	2
Dark cells					86	55	57	31								
Stoppage of diet					240	81	206	35			596	17	461	27	394	36
Whipping								1						4	2	
Put in irons/handcuffs			20								1	3				
Shipped (?)											1					
Other punishments					130	21	23	4								
Total	115	31	64	14	488	168	287	70	310	18	608	38	485	27	408	38

The punishments include solitary confinement, sometimes in dark cells, whipping, being handcuffed or put in irons, but the most common punishment was reduction or stoppage of food. One prisoner was shipped; this probably means he was sent to a hulk or a convict prison. The reasons for the punishments are not recorded, except for the 20 prisoners in irons, who took part in an attempted escape. Governor Everest stated in 1835 that the 'silent system', which was directed by the justices, had been implemented to good effect, however it was impossible to maintain silence whilst prisoners congregated in the day rooms. He reported an increase in punishments arising from enforcement of the silent system but gave no numbers.

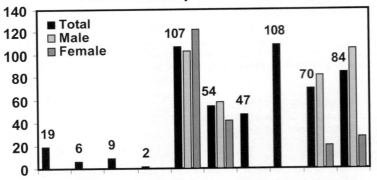

Punishments per 100 Prisoners

There is a large change in the number of punishments between the 1830s and 1840s.

There is no pattern for the number of punishments for the later years but they show that it was a hard regime in which, on average, most males and between 20-50% of the women were punished for a breach of the Rules and Regulations.

One serious prison offence was recorded in the Governor's journal:[26]

20th Jan, 1865.—A savage and unprovoked assault was made on a warder, by a prisoner undergoing imprisonment for house-breaking, and who was engaged in the stone yard. Whilst the officer's back was towards him, he struck him on the leg with a sledge hammer, used for breaking the larger blocks of stone. The warder's leg was broken, and the man's murderous intention to have again struck him on the head was providentially prevented by the gallant behaviour of another prisoner, who seized the hammer and eventually took it from the man. (Nine months of this man's punishment has been remitted by Her Majesty.)

In less than an hour the case was investigated by two Visiting Justices, and the would-be murderer committed for trial at the assizes, where he was sentenced to twenty years' penal servitude.

CHAPTER 11

Prisoners' Employment and Diet

At the end of the eighteenth century, prison was solely for the detention of offenders and not a place of punishment. This meant that the justices could allow the gaol to be used as a commercial, profit making concern. In the time of governor Chapple all prisoners could do useful work, which earned money for the county, the gaoler and the prisoner. The work for men consisted of cutting and polishing stone & slate, cutting wood, shoemaking and working in the garden. The women were employed in spinning, weaving and knitting. The gaoler would supply the raw materials and sell the finished objects. The prison workshop was a 'house of Industry', which kept the prisoners out of mischief and allowed them to earn as much as possible for their fees and maintenance and their families. Many prisoners, who had never been taught any trade before, were provided with the means of earning a livelihood after their discharge from the Prison.[54]

In the early nineteenth century the prison system came under criticism,[64] it was pointed out that it did not deter criminals from re-offending, in fact, *'under the system of profitable employment, the prison became, for many a poor labourer, a rather comfortable place. The healthy surroundings, ample but simple food, and regular employment compared favourably with his lot when out of gaol'*. It was alleged that the great increase in the numbers committed to prison was due to their positive attractiveness. This led to the suggestion that any productive labour in prison was bad, because in was too pleasant for the inmates. Useless labour was considered a great deterrent because the prisoner hated it for its uselessness; indeed, it was even argued that the knowledge that his work accomplished nothing had a reformative effect. These new ideas were accepted by the governor at Bodmin and led to the introduction of the treadwheel.

These arguments seemed to confuse the authorities and they did not know what to do with the prisoners. The 1844[12] report showed that there was unemployment in the prison. Of the 734 criminal prisoners confined during the previous year, 310 (42.2%), including 13 boys under 17 years of age, were employed at hard labour, 275 (37.5%), including 31 boys & 10 girls, had employment and the remaining 149 (20.3%) were unemployed.

In 1860,[22] many of the men were employed in the building of the new gaol but in 1865,[26] the employment reverted to servicing the prison and some trade work, for example shoemaking and tailoring. The treadwheel is not in use but oakum picking is listed and some prisoners now attend school.

After the 1865 Act, which in addition to abolishing the distinction between the

Employment of Prisoners 1860 and 1865

Year	1860	1865		1860	1865
Male Prisoners	74	74	**Female Prisoners**	32	25
Hand corn mills	3	12	At needlework	10	10
Carpentering	2		At mangling	3	2
Stone cutting	1		At washing	5	
Smiths' work	1		In the laundry	4	2
Painting	1		Cleaning	8	
Excavating	29		Cleaning / Exercising		8
Stone breaking	4		School		3
Cleaning / Exercising	25	25			
Shoemaking		2			
Tailoring		2			
Assist. Cook & baker		1			
Brush making		1			
Gardening		1			
Oakum picking		16			
School		7			
Total	66	67	**Total**	30	25

house of correction and the gaol, all prisoners had to be subjected to penal labour in prescribed form, either hard labour 1st Class on the treadwheel, the crank, the capstan or at shot drill or stone breaking or hard labour 2nd Class which consisted of any labour approved by the Secretary of State. Most prisoners started in 1st Class and after three months, became eligible to transfer to 2nd Class.

HARD LABOUR, Ist CLASS.

The treadwheel, 32 on the wheel, and 32 in waiting, working four hours and resting four hours by alternate periods of 15 minutes, ascending 7,200 feet During rest the prisoners are employed picking oakum. Rope beating and mat weaving with heavy looms, and occasional stone breaking for prison use.

HARD LABOUR, 2nd CLASS.

Rope and oakum picking, mat-making, and trades employment for males; washing, needlework and oakum picking for females.

Those who by their amenability to prison discipline, and who had served the period required by the Prison Act, 1865, at first class hard labour, were employed at mat making, and were allowed a small percentage on the whole of the quantity manufactured by them, which was paid on discharge. The system acted satisfactorily, although the numbers employed were very limited under the requirements of the Prison Act, 1865

The Inspectors Report 1875[29] contains full details of the employment of prisoners from October 1873 – September 1874.

Employment of Prisoners from October 1873 to September 1874.

Employment	Daily Average Number of Prisoners Employed			Profit on Work Done during the Year			Est. Value of Work Done for Prison			Total		
	M	F	Total	£	s.	d.	£	s.	d.	£	s.	d.
Tread-wheel	24-25			40	14	1				40	14	1
Stone-breaking	< 1						0	18	0	0	18	0
Rope picking/oakum beating	2 - 3			15	3	8	0	7	0	15	10	8
Mat-making with heavy looms	2 - 3			15	0	0				15	0	0
Digging & excavating	2 - 3						50	0	0	50	0	0
Bricklayers & masons	< 1						4	17	6	4	17	6
Rolling & repairing walks	< 1						12	3	0	12	3	0
Tailors & shoemakers	1 - 2						46	0	0	46	0	0
Painters	< 1						2	14	0	2	14	0
Carpenters & blacksmiths	1 - 2						27	16	0	27	16	0
Brush & mat makers	7 - 8			80	18	11	3	0	0	83	18	11
Oakum or coir pickers	6 - 7			20	0	0	1	0	0	21	0	0
Cleaning the prison	9 -10						35	0	0	35	0	0
Service of the prison	1 - 2						30	6	0	30	6	0
Woodcutting	< 1						2	0	0	2	0	0
Knitting & needlework		3 - 4					20	2	8	20	2	8
Wringing		2 - 3					10	0	0	10	0	0
Washing		5 - 6					43	11	0	43	11	0
Total	61-62	11-12	73-74	£171	16	8	£289	15	2	£461	11	10

The daily average number of prisoners for the same period was 75 males and 16 females. The numbers of days in the table are rounded to the nearest whole number as the fractions in the original document are illegible. The numbers confirm that approximately 80% of the inmates were employed and 20% unemployed. The productive tasks, which made profits, were treadwheel grinding corn for sale and the oakum / coir which was used to make mats and brushes. All the other employment was related to the running of the gaol, providing services and essentials, for example, shoes and knitted goods for the prisoners. At this time, most of the work was 'useful' there is little evidence of the boring, repetitive useless work ordered in the earlier Acts of Parliament. The task of oakum picking, much favoured by the government as the work was done by inmates in their cells to conform to the 'separate system', had been extended to profitable brush and mat making work.

The profits generated were very small when compared to the cost of running the institution. The total expenditure of the prison, including salaries, for the year ending 29th September, 1874 was £3,737 15s. 5d. The average for the previous five years was £3,501 11s. 10¼d. The average annual cost per prisoner was £41 1s. 5d. while the profit generated per prisoner was only £1 17s. 9d. The weekly cost of food per prisoner was £0 2s.1¾d. (less than 11 pence per week). For the year the total salary bill amounted to £923 12s. 0d. The staff consisted of 10 male warders and four sub-officers and three female warders, schoolmaster and clerks.

Sometime after 1878, the Hard labour system of the 1865 Act was changed to the *'Progressive Four Stage System'*. In this system prisoners started at hardest labour in their cells, slept on a plank and were allowed no exercise or privileges, when they had accumulated 224 points, earned at a maximum of 8 per day for being obedient and docile, they were transferred to the second stage. Similar times were spent in the 2nd and 3rd stages. The details of this system are described in the 'The Naval Prison' chapter. It is not clear how this system worked in Bodmin and other local prisons as the 'perfect prisoner' took a minimum of three months to arrive at stage four, whereas eighty-nine percent of prisoners were sentenced to less than three months imprisonment. Oakum picking was still used as hard labour, even after the time when ships were being built of iron and it could not be sold, because it could be imposed on prisoners of any physical strength or mental ability and it could be performed in silence in absolute cellular isolation.

The last major change in employment came with the Prison Act of 1898. The treadwheel and crank were abolished and all work now had to be productive. This created problems for the Prison Commissioners, who had to find work for both prisoners in association (now allowed but still to be in total silence) and also hard labour that prisoners could do in their cells. These changes created many difficulties. The goods produced could not be sold to the public as both companies and trade unions would not tolerate cheap prison labour as competitors. Therefore all goods produced were used in the prison system or other government departments. The domestic work included cleaning and maintenance of the buildings. The prison workshops made and repaired boots, clothing and various pieces of equipment. In addition, coal bag making, for use on Royal Navy steam powered warships, and mail bag sewing were introduced. These canvas goods were sold to the Forces during the Boer War (1899-1902). Bag making was a cellular activity but after one month, prisoners qualified for associated labour. The few female prisoners in the gaol worked in the laundry. The change to productive labour resulted in a profit of £1000 for the year 1901. [65]

The Use of the Treadwheel in Bodmin Gaol

The Treadwheel

The treadwheel, also known as a treadmill, was the main hard labour device used at Bodmin. The wheel, after 1870, was a revolving drum, about six foot in diameter and up to eighty foot long, having about 20-25 treadboards. This could accommodate 32 prisoners in four groups of eight. Each prisoner was screened from the next to prevent communication. The photograph, taken in Pentonville prison in 1895, shows a wheel similar in design to the Bodmin treadwheel except that the prisoners are in groups of six not eight.

www.learnhistory.org.uk

Chapple applied to the justices in October 1822 for permission to build a treadwheel. This was granted and a Bill to control the use of it was issued in 1824. The Visiting justices allowed a new, 'treadwheel without a corn mill' to be erected in the bridewell and an enlarged hand corn mill to grind sufficient corn for all prisoners in 1829. At their next visit, the justices stated that a small additional cost would allow the mill machinery to be attached to the wheel 'if desired'. Were they unsure of making the treadwheel 'useful labour' and therefore too pleasant for the prisoners? The hand mill did not supply the needs of the prison or provide adequate labour for the class of prisoners employed on it, so the two machines were united sometime before 1843.

The treadwheel was not a popular punishment, many prisoners were injured, some wounded their legs and feet, and applied poisonous metals in order to keep the wounds open, so that they might not be put to work and it even led to a riot:[66]

On Monday last, the prisoners in Bodmin prison, sentenced to hard labour, refused to go upon the tread-mill, and declared they were resolved to resist every attempt to compel them to resume their labour. Two of the visiting magistrates . . . were immediately sent for, and on their arrival they remonstrated with the rioters, but in vain; they tore up the railing that was round the wheel and arming themselves, prepared for resistance.

Finding every other means unavailing, the staff of the Cornwall Militia were called together, and being armed and provided with ammunition, were drawn up in the outer yard of the prison. As soon as their arrival was announced to the rioters, they gave three cheers, shouting— "death or victory." . . . The militia men were then directed to enter the inner yard; and as the first file were about to pass the gate, some of the most daring of the rioters attempted to wrest their muskets from them. This attack was spiritedly and successfully resisted without firing, and the rioters retreated, some of them having been knocked down by the butt end of the soldiers' firelocks, and five of the most refractory being secured, and lodged in separate cells, the others then submitted. Sowden, who was convicted at the late Truro Sessions of a violent assault on the constables of Camborne, being the ring-leader, was ordered by the magistrates to ascend the wheel, which he positively refused to do. The magistrates finding it absolutely necessary to shew the prisoners that they were resolved to enforce obedience, and to correct a notion they appear to have entertained, that the magistrates could not inflict corporal punishment on them, orders were given to flog Sowden, which were instantly carried into effect, in a manner that will for some time afford him a feeling proof of his error. The other rioters, who beheld the punishment of their leader, were then ordered to ascend the wheel, under pain of a similar infliction, when they wisely chose the lesser evil, and resumed the obnoxious operation and promised obedience.

18th May, 1827.

The 9th Report of the Inspectors of Prisons (1843) gives the following detailed description of labour on the treadwheel:-

The number of working hours per day depended on the month; December 6½; January & November 7; February & October 8; March 9; September 9½ and April - August 10. The wheel held 60 prisoners at a time, however, 90 prisoners worked on the wheel per day, one third resting or doing other work when not on the wheel. The height of each step was 7½ inches and the working rate was 48 steps per minute. This resulted in each prisoner ascending between 7,800 – 12,000 ft. per day, depending on the length of the working day. The total ascent for the wheel per day was 11,700 – 18,000 ft. This employment was for six days per week and lasted for the length of the sentence. The power generated was used for grinding corn for the Prison and the County lunatic Asylum. It is not reported which types or class of prisoners worked on the treadwheel in Bodmin but in the same year the Inspectors in the general survey stated that *'the treadmill was prejudicial to health for some prisoners and it exposes the prisoners to serious accidents.'* They stated that treadwheel labour was improper for females and boys under the age of fourteen and that it should only be used for prisoners sentenced to hard labour, and only with the permission of the Medical Officer.

The inspector of Prisons stated that in 1860 *'there is a single hard-labour machine (treadwheel) in the prison, which is only worked by men out of whom no other work can be got; it is very seldom used, but when it is, 10,000 revolutions are required in the day.'* The treadwheel was not in use in 1865 but in October, 1866, the governor reported *'some considerable progress has been made in the preparations for the new treadwheel and corn mill, sanctioned by your honourable Court, to meet the requirements of the Prison Act of 1865 '*. The new building, which cost £1,800, housed a treadwheel and corn mill. The treadwheel was finally abolished in 1898.

Oakum Picking

This consisted of unravelling pieces of old rope into individual filaments, called oakum. This was sold to ship-yards where it was mixed with tar and used for caulking wooden ships. The tarred oakum was forced between the planks to make the ship watertight. Oakum picking was extremely tedious work and was very hard on the hands. All types of prisoners, including children, were employed in this task in their cells.

The Crank

Devised in 1846, the crank was a machine which could be used in cells. It consisted of a narrow metal drum, partially filled with sand, with a handle and a counter. When the handle was turned a series of scoops inside the machine filled with the sand and when they reached the top they emptied, similar in design to a dredger. Crank labour usually meant making 10,000 revolutions at the rate of 1200 revolutions per hour; this would last eight hours and twenty minutes. The amount of sand could be varied to make the task harder or easier, depending on the physical strength of the prisoner. Although recommended by Act of Parliament for hard labour, there is no evidence that cranks were used in Bodmin.

The following extract from the Governor's journal possesses sufficient interest to be recorded in this report[26]:—

19th Nov. 1864.—Owing to the small number of female prisoners in confinement, it became necessary to select some male prisoners who could assist in the washing; four men were chosen and placed in the wash-house, without in the least degree having any communication with or having even to pass through the female department. These men washed the whole of the shirts, &c., which were then left in the wash-house to be dried and mangled by the female prisoners. This gave much relief, both on this and subsequently on one or two occasions.

Dietaries

The quantity and cost of food provided to prisoners was always a contentious issue. Many people complained that prisoners were better fed than the generally poor, local population. The authorities, who were responsible for the health of the prisoners, had to provide sufficient food to enable the prisoners to work at hard labour, without them starving. During the nineteenth century, the Home Office gradually took control of the issue and published dietaries which depended on the length of sentence and the type of work done by the prisoners.

The diet for male prisoners in 1782 was 1lb. 3oz. of 'good wholesome bread' per day and 1lb. for women. All prisoners who attended divine service on Saturday were allowed, at the county expense, ½lb. of meat made into broth for dinner on Sunday. Similar diets were reported for 1803 and 1814, although the amount of bread was stated as 1lb. 11oz. and later 1lb. 6oz.

The Gaol Act of 1823 ordered the following diet:

1. *All prisoners who are entitled by law to receive food from the County shall be provided with the following diet:-*
   Two lbs. of bread, 2 oz. of cheese and one onion for four days in the week, and 2 lbs. of bread, ¾ lb. of suet puddings, three days in the week.

2. *For prisoners under sentence of confinement, for terms not exceeding three months:—*
   Two lbs. of bread, 2 oz. of cheese, four days in the week, 2 lbs. of bread, 1 onion, three days in the week.

3. *For prisoners whose term of imprisonment does not exceed six months :—*
   Two lbs. of bread, 2 oz. of cheese, four days, 2 lbs. of bread. ¾ lb. of suet puddings, three days.

4. *For prisoners whose term of imprisonment does not exceed twelve months:*
   For the first six months as above, for the remaining term a pint of small beer three days in the week in addition.

5. *For those prisoners who shall be for twelve months and upwards.*
   For twelve months as above, and after the twelve months an additional pint of beer per week.

This dietary was ignored by local authorities and even ten years later, different gaols still had different diets. The diet at the County Gaol at Bodmin was cited for having one of the worst diets in the country.[67]

To give one instance of the contrasts in prison diet, we may adduce the Somerset House of Correction at Shepton Mallet, where, in 1833, each prisoner had, daily, one pound of bread, one pound of potatoes, six ounces of beef without bone, and one-and-a-half pints of oatmeal gruel; and, when working on the tread-mill, also a pint-and-a-half of soup, or gruel when leaving work. On the other hand, at the Cornwall County Gaol, at Bodmin, the daily ration was, for the first month, only a pound-and-a-half of bread, with the addition, after that period, of a portion of gruel.

The government persisted with the proposed changes but there was still resistance to change in Cornwall. [68]

The Chairman called the attention of the Bench to a recommendation from the Home Office for the erection in the gaol of a steam [cooking] apparatus . . . required in consequence of the alterations in the dietary . . . It was their [the magistrates'] opinion that a more unjust dietary was never passed. It was most unjust to the industrious labourer who did not get once a month so good a soup as the prisoners were to have three times a day . . . The Chairman said that the prisoners that were in gaol for a few days only were to have none of this soup—it was only those that were in for a long period, and had hard work to do. Before, the prisoners went out of gaol at the end of their confinement considerably reduced. 5 January 1844

The magistrates finally accepted the change as they had to comply with the order.

The following document[29] is dated 1874 but similar dietaries were in force before 1850.

Prison Diets for 1874.

CLASS 1: *Convicted Prisoners confined for any Term not exceeding Fourteen Days.*
Diet for all Prisoners: **Breakfast & Supper**, 1 pint of Gruel, **Dinner**, 1 lb. of bread.

CLASS 2

Convicted Prisoners confined for any Term exceeding Fourteen Days and not exceeding One Calendar Month.

	Males over 16 years of age	Males under 16, and Females
Breakfast and Supper	1 pint gruel, 6 oz. bread	1 pint gruel, 6 oz. bread
Dinner	12 oz. bread	8 oz. bread

Male Prisoners of this Class when employed at Hard Labour of the 1st. Class, to have two-thirds of a pint of soup three times a week. Women in the Laundry 4 oz. of bread additional at Dinner.

CLASS 3

Convicted Prisoners for Terms exceeding One Calendar Month, and not exceeding Two Months.

		Males over 16 years of age	Males under 16, and Females
Breakfast and Supper		1 pint gruel, 6 oz. bread	1 pint gruel, 6 oz. bread
Dinner	Sunday Tuesday Thursday Saturday	2 oz.dressed meat 1 lb. potatoes	2 oz.dressed meat 12 oz. potatoes
	Monday Wednesday Friday	⅔ pint soup 1 lb. potatoes	⅔ pint soup 12 oz. potatoes

Male Prisoners, if at Hard Labour of the 1st. Class, to have 4 oz. of Bread at Dinner. Women in the Laundry to have in addition 6 oz. Bread daily.

CLASS 4

Convicted Prisoners at Hard Labour for Terms exceeding Two Months, and not exceeding Six Months; and Convicted Prisoners not at Hard Labour for Terms exceeding Two Months.

	Males over 16 years of age	Males under 16, and Females
Breakfast and Supper	1 pint gruel, 8 oz. bread	1 pint gruel, 6 oz. bread
Dinner for 4 days	3 oz.dressed meat 1 lb. potatoes	2 oz.dressed meat 1 lb. potatoes
Dinner for 3 days	1 pint soup 1 lb. potatoes	1 pint soup 1lb. potatoes

Male Prisoners, at Hard Labour 1st. Class, to have 8 oz., and Females employed in the Laundry 6 oz. additional Bread at Dinner.

CLASS 5

Prisoners at Hard Labour whose Sentences exceed Six Months.

	Males over 16 years of age	Males under 16, and Females
Breakfast and Supper	1 pint gruel, 8 oz. bread	1 pint gruel, 6 oz. bread
Dinner for 4 days	4 oz.dressed meat 1 lb. potatoes 6 oz. bread	3 oz.dressed meat 1 lb. potatoes 4 oz. bread
Dinner for 3 days	1 pint soup 1 lb. potatoes 6 oz. bread	1 pint soup 1lb. potatoes 4 oz. bread

The above Classes to be Progressive.

Prisoners sentenced to Solitary Confinement to have the ordinary Diet of their respective Classes, without the addition for 1st Class Hard Labour.

Prisoners before Trial, when the period between Commitment and Trial.

Shall not exceed one calendar month - - - - - - - - - - - - - - -as Class 3.

Shall exceed one month, but not exceed four months - - - - as Class 4, with extra bread.

Shall exceed four months -as Class 5.

Misdemeanants of the First Division who do not maintain themselves, the same as Prisoners before Trial.

Prisoners under Punishment for Prison Offences for Terms not exceeding Three Days.

1 lb. Bread per diem.

Prisoners in Close Confinement for Prison Offences for Terms exceeding Three Days.

The Diet of Class 2.

Debtors who do not maintain themselves. The Diet of Class 4, with extra Bread.

NOTE - 4 ozs. of split peas made into a pudding may be substituted for 1 Ib. of potatoes occasionally, but the change shall not be substituted more than three times a week. The soup to contain per pint 2 ozs. raw meat without bone, 3 ozs. potatoes, 1 oz. barley, rice or oatmeal, and 1 oz. of onions or leeks, with pepper and salt. The gruel to contain 2 ozs. oatmeal per pint and be seasoned with salt.

The diet is similar to the earlier Bodmin diet consisting of bread and gruel (a very thin porridge) but after one month, meat & potato meals and soup are added. The quantity of food is increased for the longer sentences. Prisoners doing hard labour get extra bread and soup even during sentences of less than one month.

DIETARY FOR PRISONERS IN LOCAL PRISONS.

PRISONERS SENTENCED TO HARD LABOUR AND OFFENDERS OF THE THIRD DIVISON.

MEALS.	DIET A.			DIET B.			DIET C.		
	—	Men.	Women and Juvenile	—	Men.	Women and Juvenile	—	Men.	Women and Juvenile
BREAKFAST.	Daily:- Bread ...... Gruel......	8 oz. 1 pint	6 oz. 1 pint	Daily :— Bread ...... Gruel......	8 oz. 1 pint	6 oz. 1 pint	Daily :— Bread ...... Gruel...... Tea.......	8 oz. 1 pint	6 oz. 1 pint
DINNER	Sunday:- Bread ...... Porridge... Monday:- Bread ...... Potatoes... Tuesday:- Bread ...... Porridge... Wednesday:- Bread ...... Suet Pudding Thursday:- Bread ...... Potatoes... Friday:- Bread .... Porridge.... Saturday:- Bread ...... Suet Pudding	8 oz. 1 pint 8 oz. 8 oz. 8 oz. 1 pint 8 oz. 8 oz. 8 oz. 8 oz. 8 oz. 1 pint 8 oz. 8 oz.	6 oz. 1 pint 6 oz. 8 oz. 6 oz. 1 pint 6 oz. 6 oz. 6 oz. 8 oz. 6 oz. 1 pint 6 oz. 6 oz.	Sunday:- Bread ...... Potatoes... Cooked Meat, preserved by heat Monday:- Bread ...... Potatoes...... Beans ...... Fat Bacon... Tuesday:- Bread ...... Potatoes... Soup...... Wednesday:- Bread ...... Potatoes... Suet Pudding Thursday:- Bread ...... Potatoes... Cooked Beef, without bone Friday:- Bread ...... Potatoes... Soup...... Saturday:- Bread ...... Potatoes... Suet Pudding	6 oz. 8 oz. 4 oz. 6 oz. 8 oz. 10 oz. 2 oz. 6 oz. 8 oz. 1 pint 6 oz. 8 oz. 10 oz. 6 oz. 8 oz. 4 oz. 6 oz. 8 oz. 1 pint 6 oz. 8 oz. 10 oz.	6 oz. 8 oz. 3 oz. 6 oz. 8 oz. 8 oz. 1 oz. 6 oz. 8 oz. 1 pint 6 oz. 8 oz. 8 oz. 6 oz. 8 oz. 3 oz. 6 oz. 8 oz. 1 pint 6 oz. 8 oz. 8 oz.	Sunday:- Bread ...... Potatoes... Cooked Meat, preserved by heat Monday:- Bread ...... Potatoes... Beans ...... Fat Bacon... Tuesday:- Bread ...... Potatoes... Soup...... Wednesday:- Bread ...... Potatoes... Suet Pudding Thursday:- Bread ...... Potatoes... Cooked Beef, without bone Friday:- Bread ...... Potatoes... Soup...... Saturday:- Bread ...... Potatoes... Suet Pudding	6 oz. 12 oz. 5 oz. 6 oz. 12 oz. 12 oz. 2 oz. 6 oz. 12 oz. 1 pint 6 oz. 12 oz. 12 oz. 6 oz. 12 oz. 5 oz. 6 oz. 12 oz. 1 pint 6 oz. 12 oz. 12 oz.	6 oz. 8 oz. 4 oz. 6 oz. 8 oz. 10 oz. 2 oz. 6 oz. 8 oz. 1 pint 6 oz. 8 oz. 10 oz. 6 oz. 8 oz. 4 oz. 6 oz. 8 oz. 1 pint 6 oz. 8 oz. 10 oz.
SUPPER......	Daily : Bread ...... Gruel......	8 oz. 1 pint	6 oz. 1 pint	Daily : Bread ...... Porridge... Gruel......	8 oz. 1 pint 	6 oz. 1 pint	Daily : Bread ...... Cocoa......	8 oz. 1 pint	6 oz. 1 pint

Juvenile prisoners may in addition to the above diet be allowed milk, not exceeding one pint per diem, at the discretion of the Medical Officer, and juveniles on diet C may be allowed one pint of porridge in lieu of tea for breakfast.

The terms to which the above diets shall be severally applied shall be those set forth in the following table:-			
TERM.	DIET A.	DIET B.	DIET C.
Seven days and under	Whole Term	———	———
More than seven days and not more than four months	Seven days	Remainder of term	———
More than four months................................	———	Four months	Remainder of term

PRISONERS on Remand or Awaiting Trial who do not maintain themselves; Offenders of the First Division who do not maintain themselves; Offenders of the Second Division; Debtors:- DIET B, provided that they shall receive for breakfast one pint of tea in lieu of gruel, and for supper one pint of cocoa in lieu of porridge or gruel; and that when detained in prison more than four months they shall receive Diet C at the expiration of the fourth month.

ALL PRISONERS ON DAY OF FIRST RECEPTION

BREAKFAST	DINNER	SUPPER
Bread..........................8 oz. Cocoa.......................1 pint	Bread..............................12 oz. Cooked meat, preserved by heat..4 oz.	Bread........................ ...8 oz. Porridge.........................1 pint

FOR IDLE OR ILL- CONDUCTED PRISONERS

No. 1 DIET.

(a)   This diet when given for a period of three days, or less, shall consist of :-
1 lb. bread per diem, with water.

(b)   When given for more than three days it shall consist of :-
(1)   1 lb. bread per diem, with water;
(2)   B diet, according to age and sex; for alternate and equal periods of three days.

(c)   The duration of time for which this diet may be ordered shall not exceed 15 days for any single term.

(d)   No task of labour shall be enforced on any one of the days on which bread and water constitute the sole food supplied to the prisoner.

(e)   No prisoner who has been upon this diet shall be again placed upon it for a fresh offence until an interval has elapsed equal to the period passed by the prisoner on No. 1 diet.

No. 2 DIET.
For a prisoner performing a daily task of labour.

(f)   This diet when given for a period of 21 days, or less, shall be as follows:—
Breakfast.............Bread 8 oz.
Dinner...........{ 1 pint of porridge containing 3 oz. Oatmeal
Potatoes, 8 oz.
Bread, 8 oz.
Supper.................Bread 8 oz.

(g)   The No. 2 Diet ordered for a period exceeding 21 days shall consist of the above diet for the first three weeks and after the fourth week. During the fourth week prisoners shall receive B diet, according to age and sex.

(h)   The entire period for which any single term of No. 2 diet may be ordered shall not exceed 42 days.

(i)   No prisoner who has been upon this diet for a period of 21 days continuously shall be again placed on it until after the expiration of one week.

(k)   If a prisoner while on No. 2 diet should be guilty of misconduct
No. 2 diet may be temporarily interrupted, and the prisoner may be placed on No. 1 diet for a period not exceeding three days; on the expiration of the period awarded on No. 1 diet the prisoner shall resume the diet originally ordered, and the period passed upon the No. 1 diet shall count as part of the period originally awarded on No. 2 diet.

No. 118

(11585 – 21 – 10 – 11)

This document from Bodmin Town Museum is dated 1911. It appears different to the earlier documents but the food is basically the same with the addition of suet pudding, fat bacon, beans and tea. It is a more varied diet than earlier but the quantity of food provided still depended on the length of the prisoner's sentence.

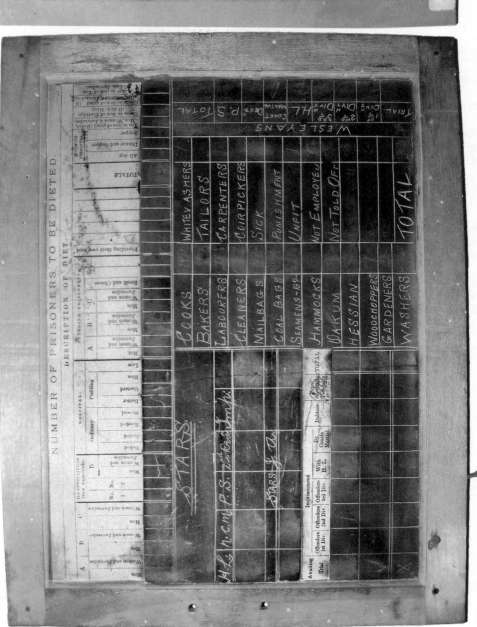

Warder's Tally Slate: Labelled 'B4 Landing', the top corridor in the Male Civil Prison. It showed the number of prisoners on that floor classified by type of sentence, for example, hard labour, court-martial, penal servitude, debtor and the class of prisoner, 1st, 2nd or 3rd Division. In addition, it recorded the numbers of prisoners on special diets, ill-conducted or idle prisoners, prisoners on hospital diets and incoming and outgoing diets. It also lists all of the different types of employment and trades.

A separate section labelled 'Wesleyans' contained the numbers of different prisoner types.

The reverse of the slate contained Cell No., Diet, Change (date of change to higher level in the 'four-stage system'?), Mattress and Discharge date.

Bodmin Town Museum

CHAPTER 12

Welfare of Prisoners

The welfare of the prisoners was the responsibility of the Chaplain, who was concerned with both religious instruction and education, and the Surgeon, who was responsible for the health of the prisoners. The objective was to improve both the spiritual and bodily health of the prisoners during their time in prison.

Education

Religious instruction, in the early days, consisted of daily chapel services and cell visits by the chaplain. This later changed to daily prayers and two services each Sunday. The cell visits were retained. Prisoners of non-established churches were visited by their own ministers. The books in the gaol, which were selected by the Chaplain, consisted of the Bible, prayer books and other moral and religious works. The main objective of the Chaplain was to get the prisoners to admit their guilt and repent and secondly, to teach the prisoners to read and write. There are a few numbers which give some indication of the size of the Chaplain's task.

State of Instruction of Prisoners						
Year	1832	1843		1846		
		M	F	M	F	
Prisoners	**684**	**474**	**138**	**428**	**155**	
Can neither Read nor Write	169	126	43	113	53	
Can Read only	198	121	61	105	73	
Can Read or Write, or both imperfectly	317	215	34	187	27	
Can Read and Write perfectly		12	0	23	2	

Of the prison population, about 30% could neither read nor write and only 35 men out of 902 and 2 out of 293 women could read and write perfectly.

The Chaplains' Reports[69] contain the following comments:

1829: *"A greater proportion of juvenile offenders...many of them were in a state of lamentable ignorance."* A Sunday school and mutual instruction enabled many to read tolerably and almost all could repeat the Lord's Prayer, the Apostles' Creed and the Ten Commandments before discharge. Some of the adult prisoners were also instructed.

1831: Prisoners willing to receive instruction but no real change of character.

1832: All prisoners, except those prevented by sickness, have attended chapel daily. Several prisoners have availed themselves of the system of mutual instruction, and have been enabled to learn to read prior to their discharge.

1833: A selection from liturgy and a chapter from bible read every morning to prisoners assembled in gaol chapel. Regular services held. On every occasion *"the whole congregation was very orderly and attentive."* Sunday school continued for juvenile offenders many of whom, *"especially parish apprentices are... in a lamentable state of ignorance".*

1834: Juvenile offenders attending Sunday School have been enabled to read fluently before discharge.

1838:[70] A school had been formed in the prison, and many boys and men had been taught to read; but the prisoner who had had the superintendence of the school had just been removed for misconduct and placed on the treadmill; and being unable to obtain another prisoner competent for the performance of the duties, the school had been suspended. The chaplain, in conclusion, urged the appointment of a permanent master to teach the prisoners.

The 31st Report[26] of the Inspectors (1866) contains the following statement:

The chaplain reads prayers every morning, gives two full services on Sundays, and administers the Sacrament once a month. He passes the mornings in visiting and instructing the male prisoners, and in the afternoon visits the females. On Saturdays he devotes his time to the debtors, and during the week frequently visits the school.

The schoolmaster has charge of the library, distributes the books, and instructs the prisoners from 10 to 12 a.m., and 1.30 to 5 p.m. daily. He also performs the duty of chapel clerk. The schoolmistress teaches daily from 2 to 4 p.m.

There is a good supply of books, both of a religious and instructive character.

From about 1870, all 'uneducated prisoners' received, on average, 6 hours secular instruction per week.

Health

Every prisoner was examined by the Surgeon, who certified that the prisoner was physically and mentally capable of performing the tasks allocated to him. If a prisoner started to lose too much weight, the Surgeon would order extra food. The number of prisoners receiving extra diet was 14 (1866), 20 (1874) and 43 in 1877.

Cases of Sickness during the course of Year												
Year	1833	1834	1835	1843		1846		1874		1877	
				M	F	M	F	M	F	M	F
Prisoners	788	549		474	138	495	166	600	132	390	139
Slight Indisposition	144		165	345	40	180	35	165			
Infirmary Cases				15	8	7	6	2	3	6	
Greatest number Sick at any one time	5	4		11	2	6	6				

Comments on prisoners' health, from various reports, are listed below:

1829:[71] Favourable report on prisoners' health. Many cases of fever occurred but not infectious or of long duration. Main diseases brought to the prison by the vagrants. Twelve on the sick list, three of whom in the infirmary, none dangerously ill.

1830:[71] Favourable report. *"The regular dietary, cleanliness and management of the Prison have prevented a recurrence of the fever which for so many years occurred at this Season"*... *"diseases principally venereal brought in by the Prisoners have been very much increased and there are several very bad cases on the sick list"*. As smallpox prevalent in neighbourhood all children and vulnerable prisoners vaccinated during last month.

1831:[71] Stated that more cases of sickness than previously, especially in June and July, with a *"flu"* epidemic.

1832:[71] Regarding health of prisoners, the introduction of the system of "Dietary and Classification", cases of fever have been reduced. Increased accommodation in the infirmary had been provided, but had not been occupied.

1832:[71] Because of the spread of cholera morbus and particularly because the disease might be introduced to the prison by vagrants from infected places, the governor, in conjunction with the Surgeon, had fumigated the gaol with the result that not one case of the disease had appeared, and the hospital had been empty for many weeks.

1832:[71] Presented most favourable report for years on prisoners' health, due to excellent management and "regular dietary". Principal diseases were among the vagrants.

1833:[71] Reported established "dietary" and extreme cleanliness resulted in not a single case of dangerous sickness among 738 persons committed.

1833:[71] Prisoners generally healthy, except during May when influenza prevailed. 144 cases of sickness during the year, only 5 at one time in the infirmary and no deaths. Mainly disease was amongst the vagrants.

1834:[71] Reported prisoners generally healthy, but several cases of fever during last three months, but no fatalities. Peter Mahon, convicted of misdemeanour, attacked with *"virulent venereal opthalmia in March last"* which did not yield to *"usual treatment"* resulting in loss of his sight. Greatest number in infirmary at any one time was four.

1835:[71] Reported 165 cases of sickness, mostly slight. Gaol free at present of infectious disease. Two patients now in infirmary - Julian, a consumptive and Ankcorn with disease of the eyes.

1838:[72] Chairman of the Cornwall Easter Sessions was sorry to say that the gaol had not been so healthy as it had previously been . . . the report of the governor attributed the illness to the use of the hand-mill now in the gaol. He (the Chairman) would only say that the hand-mill had been in use for four or five years before, and was not supposed to be injurious to the health of the prisoners. The working of it was rather easier than formerly, and the prisoners, during the last few years, were generally in good health. However there was no doubt from the opinion of the surgeon, who agreed with Mr Everest (the governor of the gaol) that their health had been affected. He did not object to the prisoners being worked hard, or to their size being diminished, but it was not intended that their health should be injured. It was the opinion of the governor, that during the late inclement season, the spare diet and the hard labour had produced the sickness.

1865:[26] The surgeon reports that the health of the prisoners has been unusually good, and no epidemic has prevailed.

1874:[29] The surgeon attends daily and oftener when necessary. He reports that the general health of the prisoners has been good; that there has been no epidemic. Light complaints are made with the view of obtaining an alteration of diet or a lightening of labour. Two males and three females have been treated in Infirmary during the year and 165 treated in their cells, of these one is on an average excused labour.

1877:[30] The surgeon attends once a day, oftener if necessary and he sees all the prisoners once a month. He states that the general health of the prisoners has been good and that there had been no epidemic disease.

Four (naval prisoners) received pardon on medical grounds. There were in all but six cases admitted into the infirmary, and during the year 72 prisoners were excused from all or part of their labour, some from infirmities existing on admission, others from temporary illness treated in cells.

1893:[55] Health and Conduct of the prisoners, male & female, has been good.

1901:[73] The general health of the prisoners has been good. No prisoner has been discharged on medical grounds. No death has occurred during the year.

Deaths in the Prison							
Year	Name	Age	Sentence	Date of Admission	State of Health	Date of Death	Cause of Death
1829	Isaac Richards				Weak		
	Mark Nicholls						Killed in quarry
	Thomas Hugo		Debtor				Ruptured blood vessel
1830	William Walkey				poor		
1831	Brown		Vagrant				
	Robert Curnow						Sudden death
1832	John Pipey		Vagrant		poor		Typhus fever
1833	None						
1834	None						
1835	Henry Lander		Vagrant		poor		Consumption
	William May		Debtor		poor		
1842	W.R.	69	Debtor	26/7/1841	Bad	28/10/1842	Diabetes
	A.T.	80	2 weeks	14/11/1842	Bad	25/11/1842	Old age
1843	E.L.	40	8 m H.L.	13/9/1842	Bad	30/1/1843	Consumption
	T.J.	16	1 y H.L.	25/5/1842	Good	8/6/1843	Fever
	W.E.	17	2 m	14/6/1842	Good	25/7/1843	Fever
1846	John H.	49	4 m H.L.	10/7/1845	Bad	26/10/1845	Angina pectoris
1874	None						
1877	?						Natural causes
	?						Natural causes
1901	None						

The above data is contained in 13 annual reports. This number of deaths (17) is very small when the total population of the gaol during the same report years totalled approximately 7,000 inmates. This death rate is significantly lower than the rate in the general population.

There were claims by prison reformers that the 'silent system' would lead to a large number of mental health problems amongst the prisoners. In Bodmin, only seven people were transferred from the gaol to the County Lunatic Asylum. J.M. (aged 39) in 1843, Joseph W. (29) in 1846, two prisoners in 1865 and three female prisoners in 1901.

Discharged Prisoners' Aid Society

The Cornwall Prisoners' Aid Society was founded sometime between 1865 and 1874. The society gave assistance to prisoners when they were discharged from prison. Forty-nine prisoners received aid in 1874 and eighty in 1877. The Society was disbanded 1916.

CHAPTER 13

Ins and Outs

This section deals with those people who must have liked life in the gaol, the re-offenders, and those who tried to leave the gaol, the escapers.

Re-offenders

The Victorians believed that their prison system was so harsh that after one visit, criminals would not want to return. Did the prison system achieve this objective?

There are statistics on recommittal rates for seven years.

Year	1830	1831	1843	1846	1865	1874	1877
Prisoners	610	552	612	661	690	732	529
Number of Reoffenders	115	89	172	184	246	189	289

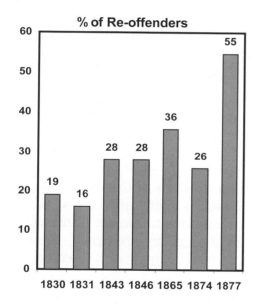

% of Re-offenders

When the numbers of re-offenders is expressed as a percentage of the total committals for the year, it would appear that recommittal rates were always high and that they increased significantly during the century. Over half of the committals in 1877 were previous inmates.

The most detailed data available is for the year 1843. In that year, 116 males and 56 females were recommitted, 85 (69m & 16f) had been in the gaol once before; 40 (22m & 18f), twice; 17 (7m & 10f), three times and 30 (18m & 12f), four times or more. There was a group of criminals who were not deterred by the life and conditions in the gaol or did they prefer to be in prison rather than out?

Escapes

The following escapes or attempted escapes have been reported in Quarter Sessions records or in *'The West Briton'* newspaper (as Published in the series *'Life in Cornwall'* by R M Barton).

1784:[74] Following attempts at escapes by prisoners at Bodmin Gaol, repairs to be carried out to the defective walls there.

1790:[75] Five militia men (in custody for not attending the 28 days required by the Militia Act), This Court highly approves of their behaviour while in custody, in preventing the escape of several convicts, and saving the lives of turnkeys and others assisting them: five guineas to be paid to the militia men, as a reward, by the vice-treasurer, out of County Stock. This order to be hung up in different parts of the gaol as an encouragement to others in a like situation.

1812:[76] Escape of two prisoners from Bodmin Gaol, August 27, 1812. George Kendall, a blacksmith, five feet ten inches high, aged 33 years, swarthy complexion, brown hair, grey eyes, a large scar on the left cheek, stout made, and one foot larger than the other. John Bayley, a travelling tinker, five feet five inches high, aged 33 years, grey hollow eyes, swarthy complexion, light sandy hair, lost two joints of his forefinger on the right hand. Whosoever will apprehend and lodge them in one of his Majesty's gaols, and give notice of the same to the gaoler of Bodmin Gaol, shall receive ten guineas reward, or five guineas for either of them.

1828:[77] Drew attention to insecure state of the bridewell, where several escapes had recently been made.

Pre 1829:[78] Parsons had previously escaped from Bodmin Gaol, having first stolen £5 from a keeper. He scaled the wall, visited a public-house, and returned to gaol of his own accord.

1831:[79] Escaped from Bodmin Gaol, early this morning, the under mentioned prisoners, charged with felony, viz.: James Medland, a native of Launceston, aged 34 years, 5 feet 9½ inches high, dark eyes, brown hair, fresh complexion, and rather bald on the top of his head; he had on, when he escaped, a fustain shooting jacket and trowsers, and a low crowned hat, with a broad brim. Thomas Hore, of St. Austell, aged 27 years, 5 feet 6 inches high, gray eyes, brown hair, fresh complexion, has a scar on his right cheek, and also near the right eye; he had on, when he escaped, a fustain jacket, striped waistcoat and corded or fustain trowsers. John Burrows, of Bodmin, aged 45 years, 5 feet 8 inches high, gray eyes, sandy hair, fresh complexion, has a scar on his forehead, is freckled and has sandy whiskers; he had on, when he escaped, a long blue frock coat, blue waist-coat and trowsers, and a glazed hat. Whoever will apprehend the said prisoners and lodge them in any of his Majesty's gaols, shall receive 5 pounds reward, for each person apprehended, on application to Mr J. B. Everest, governor of the said gaol.

1832:[69] 20 prisoners were in irons for attempting to escape.

1833:[80] Escaped from the gaol at Bodmin, this morning, the 5th of December, 1833, four prisoners, viz.—John Walters, aged 41, 5 feet 6£ inches high, grey eyes, brown hair, sallow complexion, marked with ink on the left wrist and back of the left hand with a W and a heart; he is a native of Truro, and escaped in the county shirt only. Edward May, aged 32, 5 feet 9 inches high, grey eyes, sandy hair, fresh complexion, bald on the top of the head, and sandy whiskers; he is a native of Plymouth and escaped in a county shirt and a blue flannel shirt only. Samuel Langley, aged 27, 5 feet 2 inches high, grey eyes, brown hair, pale complexion, with a large mole between the shoulders; he is a native of Winkfield, in Berkshire, and escaped in the county shirt only. Thomas Jeffers, aged 27, 5 feet 7 inches high, grey eyes, dark hair, dark complexion, marked with ink on the left arm with a ship, an anchor and a sloop, and on the right arm with a sloop; mark of a wound on the right side of the face; he is a native of Bristol, and escaped in the county shirt only. A reward of five pounds will be paid on the apprehension of either of the above men, on being safely lodged in any of his Majesty's gaols. Langley and Jeffers were recaptured in a straw-shed near Liskeard a week later. They had posed as escaped smugglers to beg for food, and were suffering badly from exposure.

1846:[13] 9th Report of the Inspectors: Joseph P. (22), a debtor, escaped and was recaptured on the 3rd May, 1864.

The only escape reported from the New Gaol was:

1890:[55] Report from Visitors Committee to Home Office. 'An officer allowed a prisoner to escape through negligence'

CHAPTER 14

The Naval Prison [81,82]

From 1872, the county gaol had been used for the detention of navy and army personnel. The Naval Prison was separated from the gaol by Admiralty Warrant and was opened in April 1887. Under the 'Naval Discipline Act' only prisoners who were to remain in the service, were imprisoned in a naval prison. Those prisoners, whose sentence included dismissal from the navy, had to be held in a civil prison. This explains the presence of naval prisoners in the civil gaol even when the Naval Prison had space.

The stated philosophy of the prison system at that time was that every prisoner should be made to feel, during the whole period of his confinement, that his state and condition in prison was worse than when he is on active service. This meant a very hard life for the prisoners. They worked hard, received basic food, were frequently reminded of their sins by the Chaplain, discipline was severe and their daily life was ruled by the 'silent system'. The governor was instructed to make arrangements that prevented all intercourse or communication between prisoners, by word or sign, so far as the business of the prison or the labour of the prisoners will permit. When working in groups, always under the supervision of an officer, communication was strictly confined to the work on which they were employed. The main objective of this regime was to prevent re-offending.

The prisoners arrived at the prison any day except for Sunday, Christmas Day and Good Friday. They would be wearing prison travelling dress or, if in uniform, would carry the following clothes; cap, jacket, trousers, shirt, pair of socks, pair of boots, braces, a flannel waistcoat, cotton or flannel drawers and a greatcoat or cloak. Every prisoner was placed in a reception cell *so that he may be strictly and minutely searched with all possible regard being paid to decency*, his clothes would be cleaned or purified, if required. An inventory of his possessions would be made, he would take a bath, his hair would be cut close and he would dress in prison uniform. If his sentence was greater than one month, his whiskers, beard and moustache would be clipped *but not so as to disfigure him.* The following morning the prisoner would be weighed, examined by the Medical Officer and was read the rules relating to the conduct and treatment of prisoners.

Every prisoner was confined in a single cell. Each cell was certified by the inspector of Naval Prisons to be of the correct size, lighted, warmed, ventilated and furnished with a means of communicating with an officer at all times. The number or mark of each cell was contained in the certificate - any changes to the cell rendered the certificate, and therefore the cell, invalid.

Prisoners wore a complete prison dress with proper marks or badges distinguishing the progressive stage to which he belonged. Every prisoner had to wash himself carefully at least once a day, and his feet at least twice a week. Each Sunday and Thursday they would be issued with a clean shirt and socks. The prisoner was responsible for all items given to him from the prison stores, any damage or loss of the items, would be paid for by the prisoner on return to his ship. The prisoners were responsible for keeping their cells, utensils, clothing and bedding clean and neatly arranged. They also had to clean and sweep the yards, passages and other parts of the prison as directed. All prisoners were compelled to attend the morning and evening Divine Services on Sundays and to take religious instruction from the chaplain, except for prisoners of denominations other than the Established Church. They had to take instruction from a minister of that church. Each prisoner was given a Bible and Prayer

Book approved for the denomination to which he belonged. Prisoners were also instructed in reading, writing and arithmetic.

Employment of Prisoners (Four Stage System)

Prisoners were not employed on Sundays, Christmas Day, Good Friday and other days appointed as Public Fasts or Thanksgivings.

Hard labour of the first class consisted of work at the shot drill, crank, capstan, stone breaking, oakum picking and any other bodily labour as may be appointed. This type of hard labour was any boring, repetitive task, which had no useful purpose. It was designed, in addition to the silent system, to break the spirit of the prisoners. Second class hard labour was defined as any bodily labour which may be appointed but it should be to the best advantage of the public service. A few prisoners of the second hard labour class, as a reward for industry and good behaviour, could be employed in the necessary services of the prison but not as warder or messenger. They were also eligible for special employment for which their services were required. The Medical Officer examined every prisoner to see if he was mentally and physically fit for the work assigned. He also, from time to time, would examine the prisoners and report the names of those *'whose health is endangered by a continuation of hard labour of a particular kind'*.

> ### Shot Drill
>
> Shot exercise performed with a 24lb shot. The shot was placed in two lines, or in the form of a rectangle, from six to eight paces apart. The men fell in, each with a shot in front of him. On a given word, the men stoop and lift the shot, so that the elbows and shot should be level with the hips, and move briskly to the next position. On a signal, the shot is placed on the floor, the man comes to attention, and, on command, marches back to his original position. This procedure is repeated for a period of 1.5hrs. The maximum for shot exercise is 3 hours per day.
>
> The whole of this exercise was timed. For example, if the shot was placed six paces apart, the shot was moved at a rate of 5 per minute. This meant that 1,800 paces were marched with the shot and 1,800 paces without shot in one hour.
>
> This exercise was changed to a punishment by increasing the shot weight to 32lbs. and changing the routine so that the prisoner did not march back to his original position but always continued to the next position. In the above example, this meant that the prisoner carried the shot for 3,600 paces in one hour.
>
> Prisoners were permitted in warm weather to remove their jackets. If a prisoner stopped during the exercise, he was to continue for 10minutes, for each stop, after the class was dismissed, unless the Medical Officer certified that it was unavoidable.

Prisoners with sentences of over 28 days entered a four stage progressive system, which was associated with length and type of work and privileges. The time spent in each stage was governed by a system of marks. A prisoner earned 6, 7 or 8 marks each working day depending on his industry. On Sunday, he was awarded with the average number of marks earned during the previous week. He remained in the first stage until he had earned 28 x 8 (224) marks. The same number of marks was required for the transitions from stage 2 to 3 and 3 to 4. The prisoner would remain in the 4th stage until his release. Any prisoner, who was idle, misconducted himself or who was inattentive to instruction, was liable to forfeit stage privileges, be detained in the stage for longer or be placed in a lower stage for a specific period.

The 1892 'Regulations for Naval Prisons', describes the rules for each the four stages. First class hard labour was only used in stage 1 and was replaced by second class hard labour for stages 2, 3 and 4. The length of the working day was gradually reduced from 10 hours (stage 1) to 8 hours (stage 4). In stage 1, the prisoner slept on a plank with no mattress, was not allowed books in his cell, lessons, exercise, library books, letters or visits. These privileges were gradually introduced in the higher stages.

In 1900, the regulations were changed to bring them into line with the regime in the Civil prison. The working day was 10 hours for all prisoners but hard labour was still restricted to stage 1. The plank was replaced by a mattress after the first fourteen days. The privileges, including library books, receiving and writing letters and visits were introduced at an earlier stage.

Details of Work and Privileges in the Four Stage System.

Year 1892	1st Stage	2nd Stage	3rd Stage	4th Stage
Hours of Work	10hr.	9hr.	8hr.(3 days) 9hr.(3 days)	8hr.
Type of Work	1st. Class hard labour. Strict separation.	2nd. Class hard labour. Strict separation.	2nd. Class hard labour. Strict separation.	2nd. Class hard labour. Strict separation.
Plank or Mattress	Plank	Mattress on 5 nights	Mattress on 6 nights	Mattress
Books in Cell	No	School & Religious	School & Religious	School & Religious
Lessons	No	No	1hr. X 3	1hr. X 6
Exercise	No	Every day	Every day	Every day
Library Books	No	No	Yes	Yes
Letters / month	No	No	No	1in & 1out
Visits	No	No	No	30min. per month
Year 1900	1st Stage	2nd Stage	3rd Stage	4th Stage
Hours of Work	10hr.	10hr.	10hr.	10hr.
Type of Work	Hard labour. Strict separation.	Less hard labour. Some association.	Less hard labour. Some association.	Less hard labour. Some association.
Plank or Mattress	Plank (1st. 14 days)	Mattress	Mattress	Mattress
Books in Cell	School & Religious	School & Religious	School & Religious	School & Religious
Lessons	No	Yes	Yes (>4hr.)	Yes (>4hr.)
Exercise	No	Every day	Every day	Every day
Library Books	No	1 per week	2 per week	2 per week
Letters / month	No	No	1 in & 1 out	1 in & 1 out
Visits	No	No	20min.on reaching stage.	30min. For each 224 marks.

The following scheme is a daily plan for Naval Prisons which have no treadwheel or crank (1892). The scheme demonstrates the improvement in prison life for those who have progressed in the four stage system.

The first stage prisoners worked from 6.30 to 8.00, 9.30 to 11.45, 1.00 to 5.35 and 6.00 to 7.45. The only breaks from the repetitive hard labour were for meals. The higher stage prisoners had more varied work, apart from the evening oakum picking, and two half-hour exercise periods a day. In addition, the 3rd and 4th stage prisoners had the evening school lessons. Sunday, apart from the two Divine Services, was a rest day for all.

TIME TABLE OF DAILY DUTIES

WEEK DAYS

A.M.

5.45	Bell rings to warn Officers to duty.
6.00	Officers come on duty. Prisoners rise, empty slops, spread out bedding to air, &c.
6.30	Labour commences.
	1st stage prisoners pick oakum in cells
	2nd, 3rd, and 4th stages, labour.
8.00	Labour ceases. Prisoners to cells for breakfast. Stow bedding, &c. Officers to breakfast, except patrols.
8.50	Officers return to duty. Patrols to breakfast.
8.55	Bell for prayers.
9.00	Prayers.
9.30	Labour recommences.

1st stage prisoners

Pick oakum in cells	9.30 to 10.15
Shot drill	10.15 to 11.45

Other stages.

Exercise	9.30 to 10.00
Labour	10.00 to 11.45

11.45	Labour ceases. Prisoners to cells for dinner.
12.00	Prisoners dinner. Officers to dinner, except Patrols.

P.M.

1.00	Officers return, to duty. Patrols to dinner till 2. Labour recommences.

1st stage prisoners

Pick oakum in cells	1.00 to 2.30

1st stage prisoners

Shot drill	2.30 to 4.00

1st stage prisoners

Pick oakum in cells	4.00 to 5.35

2nd, 3rd and 4th stages,

Exercise	1.00 to 1.30

2nd, 3rd and 4th stages,

Labour	1.30 to 5.35

4.00	Night duty Officers to tea, returning at 5.45.
5.35	Labour ceases. Prisoners to cells for supper.
6.00	Officers go off duty, except those on night duty.
	Labour recommences in cells picking oakum.

1st and 2nd stages	6.0 to 7.45
3rd stage, 3 nights a week	6.0 to 7.45
3rd stage, 3 nights a week	6.0 to 6.45
4th stage	6.0 to 6.45

6.45	School for 3rd and 4th stages.

3rd stage, 3 nights a week	6.45 to 7.45
4th stage, every night	6.45 to 7.45

7.45	Labour and school cease. Task performed in cells given out, cells cleaned, beds made.
8.00	Prisoners to bed. Lights out.

SUNDAYS

A.M.

6.15	Bell rings to warn Officers to duty.
6.30	Officers come on duty. Prisoners rise, &c.
8.00	Prisoners' breakfast. Officers to breakfast, except Patrols.
9.00	Officers return to duty. Patrols to Breakfast.
9.55	2nd, 3rd, and 4th stage prisoners, exercise.
10.25	Bell for Divine Service.
10.30	Divine Service.
12.00	Prisoners' dinner. Officers to dinner, except Patrols.

P.M.

1.30	Officers return to duty. Patrols to dinner.
2.25	2nd, 3rd, and 4th stage prisoners, Exercise.
2.55	Bell for Divine Service.
3.00	Divine Service.
4.00	Prisoners to cells.
4.30	Night Duty Officers to tea.
5.00	Prisoners' supper.
5.30	Officers go off duty. Those for night duty return.
8.00	Prisoners to bed. Lights out.

NOTE—The hours for Shot Drill and Exercise may be temporarily altered in case of any exigency of weather, &c., rendering much change necessary, and the Governor is to record all such changes in his Journal.

The Naval Prison Dietary (1892)

The following tables contain the prisoners' diets for use in Naval Prisons in England. The diet basically consisted of a breakfast consisting of oatmeal and milk, a dinner of pea or lentil flour with milk and supper of bread and milk. The basic diet was augmented, for prisoners on hard labour, by the addition of meat meals, which consisted of beef without bone, potatoes or bread, soup thickened with oatmeal and seasoned vegetables. The number of beef dinners and the quantity of some items was dependant on the length of the sentence.

SCALE 1			SCALE 2		
Dietary for first 28 days for all Prisoners undergoing hard labour, except those sentenced to 6 months or more, who will commence on Scale 2.			Dietary for after 28 days for all Prisoners undergoing hard labour, including those sentenced to 6 months or more, who will commence on this Scale.		
Breakfast	Daily	8oz. Oatmeal / ½ pint milk	Breakfast	Daily	8 oz. Oatmeal / ½ pint milk
Dinner	Tuesday Thursday	8oz. beef without bone, 1lb. of potatoes or 8 oz. bread, 1 pint of soup containing 1oz. of oatmeal, 2 oz. of vegetables seasoned with pepper / salt.	Dinner	Sunday Tuesday Thursday	8 oz. beef without bone, 1lb of potatoes or 8 oz. bread, 1 pint of soup containing 1oz. of oatmeal, 2 oz. of vegetables seasoned with pepper / salt.
	Other days	9oz. pea or lentil flour. / ½ pint milk		Other days	9oz. pea or lentil flour. / ½ pint milk
Supper	Tuesday Thursday	8 oz. bread / ½ pint milk	Supper	Sunday Tuesday Thursday	8 oz. bread / ½ pint milk
	Other days	12 oz. bread / ½ pint milk		Other days	12 oz. bread / ½ pint milk

SCALE 3			SCALE 4		
Dietary after 56 days for all Prisoners undergoing hard labour, including those sentenced to 6 months or more, who will come on to this scale after 28 days.			Dietary of Prisoners not employed at severe hard labour.		
This scale is the same as Scale 2 with the following changes: Breakfast: 10 oz. Oatmeal on 4 days. Dinner: 12 oz. of pea or lentil flour on 4 days. On Sunday, prisoners in the fourth progressive stage may have 10 oz. of beef without bone before cooking, instead of 8 oz.			Breakfast	Daily	8 oz. Oatmeal / ½ pint milk
			Dinner	Daily	6 or 9 oz.* pea or lentil flour. / ½ pint milk
			Supper	Daily	8 or 12 oz.* bread / ½ pint milk
			* The lower quantity is for prisoners sentenced to less than 56 days. The higher numbers for sentences above 56 days. If the sentence exceeds three months, one meat dinner per week may be allowed to men placed on this scale.		

When it is deemed necessary for the health of prisoners, the Medical Officer may substitute bread for oatmeal, or pea or lentil flour. 10 oz. bread for 8 oz. oatmeal. 12 oz. bread for 9 oz. of pea or lentil flour and 8 oz bread for 6 oz. of pea or lentil flour.

Punishment Diet in Naval Prisons

The standard punishment diet was 1lb. of bread daily and any quantity of water that the prisoner wanted. This diet was limited to 3 days, for longer periods the following diets were used:

No. 1 SCALE:

When given for more than three days it consists of (a) 1 lb. bread *per diem* with water and (b) the ordinary diet of the prison, for alternate equal periods not exceeding three days in duration. Thus, if the prisoner was sentenced to the No.1 scale for twelve days, he would be on bread and water for a total of six days, the bread and water days alternating with the ordinary diet in periods of one, two or three days, at the discretion of the Governor. The No. 1 scale may be ordered for any single term not exceeding 18 days. The prisoner will not work on the bread and water days.

No. 2 SCALE For prisoners not tasked at any labour: *Stirabout Diet.*

> Breakfast: Bread, 8 ounces.
> Dinner: 1 pint stirabout, containing 2 oz. oatmeal;
> 2 oz. pea or lentil flour; salt; potatoes 8 oz.
> Supper: Bread, 8 oz.

When the No. 2 scale is ordered for a period exceeding 21 days, it is to consist of the No.2 diet for the first three weeks and after the fourth week. During the fourth week the prisoner is to receive the ordinary prison diet. The entire period for which the No.2 diet is ordered is not to exceed 42 days.

No. 3 SCALE For prisoners performing a daily task of labour: *Full Stirabout Diet.*

As No. 2 scale, except Dinner: 1½ pint stirabout containing 3 oz. oatmeal and 3 oz. of pea or lentil flour; salt; potatoes 8 oz. and bread 8 oz.

When the No. 3 scale is ordered for a period exceeding 42 days, it is to consist of the No.3 diet for the first six weeks and after the eighth week. During the interval of 14 days the prisoner is to receive the ordinary prison diet. The entire period for which the No.3 diet is ordered is not to exceed 84 days.

Prison Offences and Punishments

The Naval Prison Rules (1892) contained the following 'Principles to be observed in the award of punishments'.

> *Experience having shown that discipline is not better maintained by commonly resorting to severe punishments, such punishments should be reserved for use when milder means have been tried unsuccessfully, and when it is necessary to apply them on particular occasions.*

> *It should also be borne in mind that many prisoners who have for the first time been brought under prison discipline are liable to commit offences from imperfect knowledge or understanding of what is required of them, and these offences, or the repetition of them, may be better prevented by instructing them, and causing the Officers to clearly and patiently explain the regulations or orders to which they are expected to conform, than by the two ready resort to the infliction of punishment.*

The Rules also stated that no punishments should be awarded except by the Governor or one or more Visitors and that no prisoner should be punished until he has heard the charges and evidence against him.

The Governor had the power to hear complaints against prisoners accused of the following offences:-

1. Disobedience of the prison regulations;
2. Common assaults by one prisoner on another;
3. Cursing and swearing;
4. Indecent behaviour;
5. Irreverent behaviour in Chapel;
6. Insulting or threatening language to any Officer or prisoner;
7. Absence from Chapel without leave;
8. Idleness or negligence at work;
9. Wilful mismanagement of work.

All the above acts were declared to be offences against prison discipline.

The Governor could award the following punishments:—

1. Confinement in a punishment cell. *Not to exceed 24 hours.*
2. Reduction of diet. *Limited to No.1 diet for 3 days, No.2 for 21 days and No.3 for 42 days. The highest level being reserved only for the gravest kinds of misconduct.*
3. Degradation to a lower stage. *Not to exceed 14 days.*
4. Prolongation of period in a stage. *Not to exceed 14 days.*
5. Deprivation of stage privileges.
6. Placing in irons, or other mechanical restraint. *This includes Handcuffs, Loose Canvas Restraint Jacket, Leg Chains or Cross Irons, Body Belt or Light Steel Connecting Chains. If the restraint was used for over 24 hours a written order from a Visitor was required, stating the cause for the restraint, the time that the prisoner was to be kept in irons and, in the case of handcuffs, whether they are to be kept in front or behind.*

The following are the punishments which could be awarded by the Visitors:—

1. (a) Imprisonment for offences under Sect. 82 Naval Discipline Act.

    This section covered interruption of a Prison Officer in the execution of his duty, or aiding or inciting any person to assault, resist or interrupt any such Officer. This case was heard before at least three of the Visitors or two Justices of the peace. The sentence was up to 6 months, with or without hard labour, provided that the sentence together with former sentence should not exceed a total period of two consecutive years imprisonment.

   (b) Corporal punishment.

    The following offences rendered prisoners to corporal punishment:—

    Mutiny, or open incitement to mutiny in the prison; Personal violence to any Officer of the prison; Aggravated or repeated assault on a fellow prisoner; Repetition of insulting or threatening language to any Officer or prisoner; Wilfully and maliciously breaking the prison windows, or otherwise destroying the prison property; When under punishment, wilfully making a disturbance tending to interrupt the order and discipline of the prison; And any other act of gross misconduct or insubordination requiring to be suppressed by extraordinary means.

    Corporal punishment was inflicted with a cat-o'-nine tails or, in the case of a boy under 18, with a birch rod, and the instruments in both instances had to be of a pattern approved by the Admiralty. The punishment should not exceed 25 lashes or strokes.

The Visitors could also award:—

2. (a) Confinement in a punishment cell. *Not to exceed 14 days.*
    (b) Degradation to a lower stage. *Not to exceed 28 days.*
    (c) Prolongation of period in a stage. *Not to exceed 28 days.*

By 1900, the number of prison offences had increased to seventeen.

1. Disobeys any order of the governor or of any other officer, or any prison regulation.
2. Treats with disrespect any officer or servant of the prison, or any visitor, or any person employed in connexion with the prison or works.
3. Is idle, careless, or negligent at work, or refuses to work.
4. Is absent without leave from divine service, or prayers, or school instruction.
5. Behaves irreverently at divine service or prayers.
6. Swears, curses, or uses any abusive, insolent, threatening, or other improper language.
7. Is indecent in language, act, or gesture.
8. Commits a common, assault upon another prisoner.
9. Converses or holds intercourse with another prisoner without authority.
10. Sings, whistles, or makes any unnecessary noise, or gives any unnecessary trouble.
11. Leaves his cell or other appointed location, or his place of work, without permission.
12. In any way disfigures or damages any part of the prison, or any article to which he may have access.
13. Commits any nuisance.
14. Has in his cell or possession any article he is not allowed to have.
15. Gives to or receives from any prisoner any article whatever without leave.
16. In any other way offends against good order and discipline.
17. Attempts to do any of the foregoing things.

All the above punishments were still used and, in addition, the governor could deprive an idle prisoner of his mattress for three days. Some offences could now result in forfeiture of seven days remission.

For the more serious offences, including personal violence to a fellow prisoner: grossly offensive or abusive language to any officer or servant of the prison; wilfully or wantonly breaking the prison windows, or otherwise destroying the prison property; when under punishment, wilfully making a disturbance tending to interrupt the order and discipline of the prison; any other act of gross misconduct or insubordination requiring to be suppressed by extraordinary means or escaping or attempting to escape from prison; the Visitors could order the same punishments as in 1892 but the severity of the punishments was increased. For example, the limits on reduction of diet had changed to: Diet No.1 for 15 days; No.2 for 42 days and No.3 for 84 days. Corporal punishment was still available for serious offences, for example mutiny, but the Admiralty had to be informed. The maximum number of strokes inflicted on the prisoner had increased from 25 strokes to 36.

Discharge of Prisoners

A prisoner, wearing his travelling dress, was discharged from prison at 7 a.m. on the day on which his sentence expired, except when that happened on a Sunday, Christmas Day or Good Friday, In that case, he was discharged on the previous day at an hour that would enable the Officer in charge of him to return to his duty on the same evening. Before his discharge a prisoner was examined by the Medical Officer and his state of health recorded. The Medical Officer also examined prisoners about to transfer to another place of confinement. In this case he would certify that the prisoner was free from malignant or infectious disease and in a fit state to be moved. On his discharge to his Ship or Division, a report on the prisoner's conduct was made to his Commanding Officer. The prisoner would receive the letters addressed to him during his time in custody with his other property, unless the Visitor should approve of the Governor withholding them on account of their content.

Part of a Civil Prison discharge document recording two naval prisoners who were D.S. (discharged from the Service). *Bodmin Town Museum*

85

Executions in Bodmin

1785	7th Mar.	**Phillip Randall**, 27, burglary in Truro.
	23rd Mar.	**R. Brown**, 33, murder of a boy.
	29th July	**William Hill**, 33, murder of John Pascoe.
	7th Aug.	**John Richards**, 25, robbery with violence from Peter Jane.
1786	6th Apr.	**Thos. Roberts**, 34, stealing 3 sheep, the property of Stephen Polkinghorne.
	26th Apr.	**Francis Coath**, 45, stealing an ewe sheep.
1787	10th Apr.	**James Elliot,** 35, highway robbery (of the mail).
	10th Apr.	**John Gould**, 23, burglary at Budock.
	20th Aug.	**William Congdon**, 23, stealing a watch.
1791	31st Mar.	**Michael J. Taylor**, 22, stealing a mare.
	31st Mar.	**John Dash**, 23, burglary.
	31st Mar.	**James Simons**, 25, stealing an ox.
	2nd Sept.	**Ben Willoughby**, 20, ⎤ murder of J.James, innkeeper Helston. **John Taylor**, 26, ⎦
	15th Sept.	**William Moyle**, feloniously stabbing and killing a mare.
1793	20th Mar.	**William Trevarevas**, 25, murdering Martha Bluett.
1795	9th Apr.	**James Frederick**, robbing and threatening Sarah Jane.
	27th Aug.	**Joseph Williams**, 28, sheep stealing.
1796		**G. A. Safehorne**, murder of a Dutchman.
	11th Aug.	**'Wild Cat' John Hoskin**, highway robbery with violence.
1798	13th Sept.	**William Howarth**, 24, stealing a purse containing 20 guineas.
1801	13th Apr.	**William Roskilly**, 34, housebreaking.
1802	25th Aug.	**Richard Andrews, alias Rowe**, forgery.
	1st Sept.	**John Vanstone**, 37, ⎤ burglary in the house of Walter Oke. **William Lee**, 60, ⎦
1804		**Joseph Strick**, 25, murder
1805	17th Apr.	**John Williamson**, 32, ⎤ breaking into the shop of Miss Tyeth. **James Joyce**, 27, ⎦
1812	13th Apr.	**Pierre Francois LaRoche** (a frenchman), 24, forging a £2 note.
	1st May	**William Wyatt**, 40, drowning Isaiah Falk Valentine, a Jew, at Fowey.
1813	6th Sept.	**Elizabeth Osborne**, 20, setting fire to a corn stack.
1814	31st Mar.	**William Burns**, 21, murder of John Allen, of Sennen.
1815	31st Mar.	**John Simms**, a soldier, murder of Joseph Burnett.
1818	--- ---	**William Rowe**, 41, sheep stealing (not on record).
1820	12th Aug.	**Sarah Polgrean**, 34, *from Gulval,* murder of her husband by poison.
	5th Sept.	**Michael Stephens**, 27, killing a ram and stealing part of its Carcase.
1821	2nd Apr.	**John Barnicott**, 24, ⎤ murder of William Hancock, at Cury. **John Thompson**, 17 ⎦
	10th Sept.	**Nicholas James Gard**, 42, murder of Thomas Hoskin.
1825	7th Apr.	**William Oxford**, 21, setting fire to a corn stack.
1827	19th Apr.	**James Eddy**, 29, robbing Jane Cock with violence and stealing 7s 0d.
1828	8th Aug.	**Elizabeth Commins**, 22, murder of her male child.
	21st Aug.	**Thomas Pring Coombe**, 21, housebreaking, 2 cases.
1834	21st Aug.	**William Hocking**, 57, bestiality.
1835	30th Mar.	**John Henwood**, 29, parracide.
1840	13th Apr.	**William Lightfoot**, 36, ⎤ for the murder of Mr Norway. **James Lightfoot**, 23, ⎦
1844	12th Aug.	**Matthew Weeks**, 23, murder of Charlotte Dymond at Roughtor.
1845	11th Aug.	**Ben Ellison**, 61, murder of Mrs Elizabeth Ruth Seman, at Penzance.
1854	3rd Apr.	**James Holman**, 27, murder of his wife Phillipa, at Crowan.
1856	11th Aug.	**William Nevan**, 44, murder of Serjeant-major Robinson, at Maker.
1862	18th Aug.	**John Doidge**, 28, murder of Roger Drew, near Launceston.
1878	15th Aug.	**Selina Wadge**, 28, murder of her child at Altarnun.
1882	13th Nov.	**William Bartlett**, 46, murder of a child at Lanlivery.
1901	9th July	**Valeri Giovanni**, 31, murder on the high seas.
1909	20th July	**William Hampton**, 24, murder of Emily Tredrea at St. Erth.

Bodmin Town Museum.

CHAPTER 15

Executions at Bodmin

In the 1770s, it was estimated that there were 241 offences for which the Assize Court could order the death penalty. Between 1785 and 1820, prisoners were hanged at Bodmin for a range of offences including burglary, robbery with violence, sheep stealing, highway robbery, stealing (including a watch, a mare, an ox and wheat), killing animals, house & shop breaking, forgery and arson. Only twelve of the thirty-six hangings were for murder. In the 1820s, Robert Peel's Prison Reform Acts greatly reduced the number of capital offences and further reforms meant that by 1860, few offences, including murder and treason, carried the death penalty. From 1821 to 1909, there were 17 hangings, 13 for murder and one each for arson (1825), highway robbery (1827), house breaking (1828) and bestiality (1834). This was the last hanging at Bodmin for an offence other than murder. There were 56 executions at Bodmin between 1785 and 1909. This number is much smaller than the number of prisoners sentenced to death by the courts. For example, the Summer Assizes held at Bodmin on the 7th August, 1820, sentenced seven prisoners to death. However only one, Sarah Polgreen, was hanged, the others were probably transported, sent to hulks or sentenced to long periods in gaol.

Sentences of the Prisoners

On Monday, August 7, 1820.

John Husband, 21, *John Carlyon*, 24, committed March 24, 1820, charged on suspicion of having wilfully, maliciously, and unlawfully stabbed and cut James Lawrey and Isaac Nicholls.——*Acquitted.*

John Penwarn, 21, *Thomas Kent*, 15, *Henry Williams*, 14, committed March 31, 1820, charged with having burglariously broken and entered the dwelling-house of James Brydges Williams, esq. and Humphry Williams, esq. and feloniously stolen a Writing Desk, sundry Bank Notes, and Cash, of the value of one hundred pounds.——*Death.*

Michael Stephens, 27, committed April 19, 1820, charged with having killed a Ram Sheep, and stolen part of the carcase, the property of Hart Nickel.——*Death.*

Edward Bennett, 27, committed April 29, 1820, charged with having ravished Elizabeth Hender.——*Acquitted.*

John Kitt, 22, committed May 3, 1820, charged with an assault and an attempt to commit a Rape on Elizabeth Penberthy.——*Six months Imprisonment and Whipped.*

John Kendall, 26, committed June 9, 1820, charged with breaking and entering the dwelling-house of John Tamblyn, and stealing three Promissory Notes for payment of one hundred pounds each, and two Gold Rings.——*Death.*

William Brouse, 21, committed July 4, 1820, charged with entering the dwelling-house of Daniel White, and stealing a Silver Watch, a Coat, and sundry articles of Wearing Apparel.——*Death.*

Eliza Annear, 17, committed July 11, 1820, charged on suspicion of the murder and concealment of the birth of her female Bastard Child.——*No bill.*

Isisdort Lambert, 20, *Gosephe Tiraut*, 23, *Geneveare Lambert*, 22, *Carolene Avie*, 22, committed July 20, 1820, charged with stealing a Shirt, the property of Ann Thomas.——*Isisdort Lambert, one month Imprisonment. The others Acquitted.*

James Hambly, 42, committed July 31, 1820, charged with stealing a quantity of Fishing Net, the property of Abraham Hambly, esq.——*Seven years Transportation.*

Sarah Polgrean, 37, committed August 1, 1820, charged on the Coroner's Inquest with the Murder of her late husband, Henry Polgrean.——*DEATH.*

Robert Bowden, 26, committed May 21, 1820, charged with stealing a pair of Shoes, the property of William Dyer, and a Hemp Sack, and sundry other articles, the property of Samuel Cawker.——*Four months Imprisonment.*

Samuel Dettis, 46, committed June 30, 1820 charged with having committed Bestiality.——*Twelve months Imprisonment and Whipped.*

John G1⌇⌇54, committed July 13, 1820, charged with having attempted to commit Bestiality.——*No Bill.*

F. ⌇mons, Printer, Bookbinder, and Stationer, opposite the Market-house, Redruth

The Place of Execution

The place of execution was moved several times during the gaol's history. Several versions of the *'Executions in Bodmin'* list, with notes on the place of execution, have been published. Abstracts from two of the lists are compared below.

Bodmin Town Museum:

1785-1821:	By gibbet in public on Bodmin Common,
1825-1862:	By drop gallows in public outside gaol.
1878-1882:	Gallows now screened from view.
1901-1909:	Scaffold and drop placed inside gaol.

In *'Bodmin Gaol'* by Alan Brunton[65]:

1785-1802:	On Bodmin Moor (St. Lawrence site).
1802-1815:	On Bodmin Moor or outside wall of the old gaol.
1820-1862:	Public hanging outside the wall of the gaol.
1878-1882:	Executed inside the new gaol in private.
1901-1909:	Executed in private inside the execution shed.

The only agreements between the two lists are that the earlier hangings took place on Bodmin Common (near St. Lawrence site), that some took place outside the gaol wall and that the last two executions were in the execution shed.

The Sherborne Mercury (August, 1796) states that the execution of Hoskin took place on Bodmin Common. The executions of Vanstone & Lee (1802) were the first by drop gallows in Cornwall. From the timings in the report, it would seem that the new drop was situated outside the gaol wall (Cornwall Gazette, 4th September, 1802). Further reports from the 1805 and 1812 executions state that the drop was *'erected without the prison wall'* and *'in front of Bodmin prison'*.

In the Quarter Sessions records for 1830/1831, the Governor reported a new execution drop was to be built over the gatehouse. This is confirmed by the painting, entitled *'An execution at Bodmin Gaol, 1841'* [18] and a much later newspaper report,[83] which states: **'Above the arched door of the gaol entrance was another, smaller door for the Chaplain, culprit and hangman to come through; outside of this were iron gratings (the trap) to walk on, with rails around to prevent the murderer from jumping off.'**

Therefore, from about 1832 until the closure of the old gaol in 1860, executions took place above the gatehouse of the old gaol.

The Inspector of Prisons noted[22] in 1861 that *'The apparatus called "the drop" for capital executions, which had inadvertently been so placed as to be nearly invisible from the exterior of the prison, had been ordered to be removed to a more suitable position.'*

The details of the next hanging, that of John Doidge in 1862, is described in detail in *'The West Briton'*, dated 22nd August: [84]

About half-past eight on Monday morning, the carpenters commenced the erection, on the principal floor of the female department of the gaol, steps and a platform inside the southern wall of the prison—the platform being on a level with the grating floor of the drop on the exterior; and at ten o'clock these preparations were completed. The drop has the same southern aspect, and is nearly over the same site as that of the old gaol: and, consequently, the fields sloping down from the northern side of the street at the western part of the town—the "Bodmin highlands"— afford the same facilities for view of the dread spectacle that have been available to so many thousands at previous executions. We understand that it had been intended, in the building of the new gaol, to erect the drop at the northern part; but this purpose was abandoned because of the comparatively small assemblage of the public to whom the execution of a capital sentence could be made visible. [The female department was the building later known as the Naval Prison.]

An Act of Parliament of 1868 ruled that executions must be screened from the public. The next two hangings, those of Selina Wadge and William Bartlett, took place out of the public view but probably at the normal execution place. A report of the Bartlett hanging in 1882 states[85] *that 'the drop was erected in an angle of the outside of the prison facing up the lane to Town Wall and down towards Dunmere. It was a wooden erection, looking at a distance like a roadman's hut. There was nothing else to be seen, but at 8 a.m. a black ball was run up by the big chimney, which spread out to be the black flag.'* The last two hangings, Giovanni (1901) and Hampton (1909) took place in the execution shed, which was built inside the gaol after 1882.

The executions on the list (page 86) were carried out at the following places:-

1785-1802:	By gibbet, on Bodmin Common (St. Lawrence site).
1802-1828:	By drop gallows outside wall of the old gaol.
1834-1856:	New drop gallows above the old gaol gate.
1862:	Drop placed on the outside of the South wall (new gaol).
1878-1882:	As above but screened from public view.
1901-1909:	Executed in private inside the execution shed.

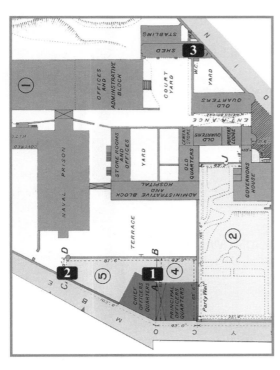

Diagram showing the three Places of Execution on the gaol site.
1. 1834 – 1856 (7 executions)
2. 1862 – 1882 (3 executions)
3. 1901 – 1909 (2 executions)

Renovated execution shed, with the cross and hanging beam.

Recently excavated pit.
Behind the wall was a staircase to allow the surgeon to enter the pit to confirm the death.

The following documents are new reproductions of contemporary broadsheets, some relating to Bodmin executions:

Life, Confession and Execution of Sarah
Polgreen (1820)
(CRO X/106/36)

Confession, Dying Behaviour and Execution of
James Eddy (1827)
(CRO X/106/42)

The Last Words of William and James
Lightfoot (1840)
(CRO X/364/5)

Horrible Murder of Elizabeth Rous Seman
(1845)
(CRO X/106/40)

Trial and Sentence of the Soldier William
Nevan (1856)
(CRO X/369/3)

Wilful murder by Joseph Williams of his wife
(Coroner's Court)   (1860)
(CRO X106/38)

(The references are the Cornwall Records Office
numbers of the original documents)

An Account of the
LIFE, CONFESSION, AND EXECUTION OF
Sarah Polgrean,

Who was convicted of causing the death of her late husband Henry
Polgrean, by poison, at the Summer Assizes, held at
Bodmin on Thursday the 10th
of August 1820.

And who was executed at BODMIN, on Saturday the 12th.

Sarah Polgrean *was born of poor parents, in the parish of* Gulval, *about the year 1786 or 1787. Her father was killed by an accident, in London. Her Mother deserted her when 4 months old, and left her chargeable to the Parish. She had no education, not being able to read or write. She was apprenticed at 9 years of age and during her apprenticeship yielded to the seduction of a fellow servant. After her time expired she lived in many places, but never settled in any of them; and about 10 years since she left Cornwall, to join her Mother at Dock, who was an in different character, and is since dead, She lived in Dock a few months, where she had some religious impressions, and married a soldier, who took her into the neighbourhood of London. Her husband and she parted by mutual consent, and she returned first to Dock, and afterwards to Cornwall, where she met with the late H. Polgrean, and married him.*

She was convicted, on the clearest evidence, of purchasing arsenic, at Penzance, for the alledged purpose of poisoning rats, though it was proved the house had never been infested with them. The surgeons and other witnesses proved the illness of the deceased, and the prisoner's concealment of it: they also proved that he had died by poison, having examined the contents of the stomach, after the body of the deceased had been disinterred, although he had been buried eleven days. It was also proved that they had lived unhappily together, and that she had threatened to poison him. The deceased had been sick on the Friday evening, and was bled on Saturday by the Surgeon, in consequence of his dinner and supper disagreeing with him on the preceding day. This agrees with the evidence of the surgeon, who thought the poison had not been administered when the deceased was bled

The judge recapitulated the evidence with great precision; and the jury without hesitation pronounced a verdict of GUILTY. -- His Lordship then proceeded to pass the awful sentence of the law, and ordered the prisoner to be executed on Saturday morning, and her body to be given for dissection. — The wretched prisoner was so overwhelmed by her dreadful fate, that she seemed to be quite insensible, and was obliged to be supported during the time sentence was passing — she was carried out of the court.

The prisoner has confessed that she mixed the arsenic in a piece of butter, taken from a half pound, on Saturday afternoon, the 15th of July; that at supper-time she proposed to her husband to eat the piece already cut off, and buttered his bread with it, whilst she eat from the larger piece herself. She attributed her crimes to the want of a religious education, and her early seduction. She solemnly declared that she was not instigated to commit the crime by any man, and that his well-founded jealousy and her aversion to him induced her to do it. She expressed her free forgiveness of all whom she conceived to have injured her, lamented, after her trial, the expressions she had uttered towards some of the witnesses against her, and hoped that her end would be a warning to all who might be tempted to commit such crimes as hers, especially those of adultery and murder.

About a quarter past twelve she was drawn upon a hurdle to the drop, amidst an immense crowd of spectators, walked to the platform with a firm step, and for a few minutes joined very audibly in prayer. After this she sung a hymn with most extraordinary resolution, and begged all present to take a solemn warning from her untimely fate, shook hands with a man at the drop, and also with the executioner, gave the signal, and was launched into eternity.

Brougham, Printer, Falmouth.

Confession, Dying Behaviour,

AND

EXECUTION

OF

James Eddy

WHO WAS

HUNG AT BODMIN,

On Thursday, the 19th of April, 1827,

PURSUANT TO HIS

Sentence at the LENT ASSIZES, for Robbing and Violently Assaulting JANE COCK, on the King's Highway.

I am twenty-nine years of age, was born in the parish of Wendron, near the borough of Helston, in the county of Cornwall; am the son of an industrious miner, and one of ten children. When I was about ten years old I went into husbandry service, and until the age of nineteen I bore, a good character. From that period I became a miner at Crinnis, and still lived in fair repute till about twenty-five. I then stole a bundle of Laths, for which I was committed to the county Gaol, was tried at Sessions, and sentenced to six weeks imprisonment. After my discharge I went to St. Blazey, and then began bad habits,—smuggling—sabbath-breaking—adultery—drinking—pilfering—gaming—wrestling—&c, and thus got a bad name. In consequence of endeavouring to injure some excise officers with gunpowder, I left St. Blazey and went to live at Redruth. In February last I came up to St. Blazey on business, and on my return met Jane Cock, by whose evidence I am condemned to die, though I solemnly declare I never robbed her or intended to rob her. I forgive all my fellow-creatures, and humbly hope through the merits of Jesus Christ, to obtain pardon of my sins, and be received into His kingdom. I die in peace with all, and forgive all that swore against me."

Immediately after his condemnation at Launceston, he was removed to the Gaol at Bodmin, where he was attended by the Rev. Mr. Boor, the Ordinary, who was unremitted in his endeavours to awake him to a sense of his lost and fallen condition. We are happy to say, that his labours appear to have been successful, the unfortunate man having evinced a readiness to be instructed in divine things, about which he was before totally ignorant and unconcerned. The confession above was taken in writing from his own words, the day before his execution, at which time he appeared truly penitent and resigned. He married early in life, and has left a wife and three small children to lament his untimely end. The night before his execution, he slept soundly, and in the morning partook of a hearty breakfast.

After receiving the sacrament in the chapel, the unhappy man walked to the place of execution, at half past eleven. He then addressed, the multitude around in nearly the following words:—" I am come to the close of my life. I acknowledge that every word which the witnesses said on my trial was true, except what Jane Cock said; the only true word which she swore to was the day of the month. All the rest was false. 'Tis true we did break the seventh commandment; but I never robbed her. Thank God! I die innocent. This is a great relief to me. I confess I have been a great sinner, and I attribute my present fate to leaving my wife and family, and following other women. I never robbed Jane Cock; and I wish I could express to you the feeling the knowledge of my innocence gives me at this moment. I die happy."— The prisoner then knelt down, and devoutly joined in prayer, at the conclusion of which he again said:—"If any person here should see Jane Cock, I hope he will talk to her of the awful consequence that her words have brought me to. If she did lose seven shillings and her pocket, some person must have found it; and I hope, whoever has found it, will bring it forward, and clear my children from this disgrace. My earthly judge thought me guilty, but he could not see my heart. I forgive him; and I hope in a few minutes I shall be in the presence of that Judge who knows me innocent. God bless you all!!!"—He shewed uncommon fortitude throughout the dreadful period, and shook hands with several of his comrades whom he recognised among the crowd. At a quarter before twelve the drop fell, and after a few struggles the world closed on him forever!!!

The place of execution was crowded beyond any thing we had ever before witnessed; and, as usual, *disgraced* with an spectacle abundance of females, whose levity of demeanour ill-accorded with the appalling. We fear that such scenes add little to the cause of morality; instead of acting as warnings to the unprincipled and vicious, we have generally found them degenarate into wantonness and riot.

F. Symons, Printer, Bookbinder, and Stationer, opposite the New Market Place, Redruth

WILLIAM LIGHTFOOT, AGED 26.   JAMES LIGHTFOOT, AGED 23.

THE LAST WORDS

OF

WILLIAM AND JAMES LIGHTFOOT,

Who were HANGED at BODMIN, on Monday April 13th, 1840,

FOR THE

WILFUL MURDER of Mr. NEVELL NORWAY,

OF WADEBRIDGE

About Five minutes before they were executed, and while the Rope was about their necks, and the Cap over their faces, William Lightfoot desired the Rev. Francis Cole, who was in attendance with some other Clergymen, to come near, and spoke to him as follows:— "Tell my wife and family that I die happy, — beg them to go, " to Church and keep the Sabbath ; — not to go in the way that I have gone, and " brought myself to ruin — Tell them to avoid idleness, and get their living honestly, " and pray that they may meet me in Heaven." After which Mr. Cole turned to James Lightfoot, and asked him if he had any thing more to say ? he, following up his Brother's words, answered, " Say that I am happy — They " (meaning his wife and child) ' must pray to God that we may meet in Heaven. "Immediately after, the Drop fell, and their souls were launched into eternity. May God be   mer ciful to them, for the sake of Jesus Christ our Lord!

Reader! If you are now living without God in the world, as   did before their apprehension,—breaking the Sabbath, —leading "disorderly lives ; — if you are the companion of Poachers, Thieves, and Oh ! break from your evil courses, and the bad companions who e them, while the day of Salvation remains ; lest the Great Enemy o   ul should unawares lead you into some dreadful sin against God, and time should yet be allowed you to make your peace with Him; before you are summoned into His presence!

Reader!— If you are a Parent or Master of a Family, be admonished by the Lightfoot's fate, to bring up your children and apprentices to know their Creator in the days of their youth ; — teach them to pray night and morning ; — oblige them to attend the Public Worship of God on the Sabbath ; — send them to the Day or, at least, the Sunday School, to be instructed in their faith and duty; — correct them betimes for lying and swearing; — see that they keep early hours and avoid bad company. So will you keep them from the clutches of the Devil, and save their Souls alive!

[KNA   INTER, WADEBRIDGE]

HORRIBLE
MURDER
Of Elizabeth Rous Seman,
Rosevean Road, Penzance,
Committed on Monday, July the 7th, 1845.

Just as we had finished our report of the festivities of Monday, we found it to be our duty to turn to a matter of the most tragical description. Whilst the thousands that were revelling in the joyous scene which we have elsewhere described—one of the most brutal and inhuman Murders must have been committed that has ever fallen to our lot to record.

In the present state of the proceedings, we forbear from furnishing our readers with the detailed evidence that was adduced, for obvious reasons; but we see no reason why we should not state briefly the particulars relating to this most diabolical act.

It appears, then, that a man residing in one of the Cottages situate in Rosevean Road, and nearly opposite the Catholic Chapel, called Benjamin Ellison, aged about 55, and of respectable appearance, called at the Temperance Hotel, in Prince's Street, kept by Capt. Edward Thomas, about eleven o'clock on Monday night, & asked for some refreshment. Subsequently he enquired if he could sleep there that night. He was answered in the affirmative, and asked how it was that he was going to stay out—why he did not go home. He replied that it was then too late—and requested to see a man called Wm. Eddy, who lodged at the Hotel. Eddy was sent for, and Ellison told him he had something important to communicate to him, and appeared rather restless—but he said nothing more than enquired of Eddy which place he preferred, Liverpool or Manchester. Eddy, in the course of conversation, asked Ellison how Mrs Seman was--(meaning the unfortunate woman who was afterwards found murdered, and with whom Ellison lived.) He said she was unwell, and then there was a pause in the conversation, which was broken by Eddy asking Ellison what it was he had to communicate to him; but nothing particular was said. Ellison appeared depressed in spirits & kept on examining and rubbing his hands. Shortly afterwards both retired to their respective places of rest.

Between five and six o'clock on the following morning, a son of Capt. Thomas's, at the Temperance Hotel, saw Ellison down stairs, who said that he wished to have his boots cleaned. He was requested to take them from off his feet for the purpose, but declined, and directed that they might be cleaned on. The boots were cleaned accordingly and the person who performed the task, represents the boots to have been very wet—as though they had been washed—but it rained pretty smartly on Monday night for some time.

He left the hotel before six o'clock, had his hair cut and got shaved—and in the course of the morning called at the house of a Mrs Hill, who resided in Rosevean Road, and informed her that his house had been broken open and that Mrs Seman had been murdered. Mrs Hill exclaimed—Good God! and accompanied him to the fatal spot. There stretched out upon the floor lay the mutilated remains of the unfortunate woman—her face was covered by a gauze veil, and marks of blood were perceptible in all directions. Ellison said he would fetch the police, & requested Mrs Hill to make an alarm.

About nine o'clock, Ellison was again at the Temperance hotel—communicated the dreadful fact, and asked Capt. Thomas to go with him to Mr. Carne, one of the magistrates.

In the mean time, the police officers were on the *qui vive*—and used the necessary precautions to secure the man on whom suspicion rested. John Martin went to the Mayor's, and while there, an individual entered, who said his name was Ellison, upon which Martin took him into custody on suspicion.

As speedily as practicable, a Coroner's Inquest was held upon the body, before JOHN ROSCORLA, ESQ., Coroner, and a respectable jury, which occupied between 8 and 9 hours. During the whole of the time, the Hall was crowded—but we think it proper to remark that although the most intense interest was excited, there was none of that feeling exhibited against Ellison which we have often stated to have occurred elsewhere when prisoners have been examined upon similar charges.

MESSRS. MILLETT and BORLASE attended the inquest on behalf of Ellison, who is stated to have said that a gold watch and wearing apparel to a considerable amount had been stolen from the dwelling—that deceased was in the receipt of an annuity—that she was about shortly to be married to a gentleman of title, and that she had agreed to settle an annual income upon him (Ellison) as soon as that event should take place.

After a short consultation, the jury returned a Verdict of *Wilful Murder* against Ellison, who was committed to Bodmin to await his trial on the charge at the next assizes.

We deem it proper to observe that neither the accused nor deceased were Cornish people—and that the awful deed cannot possibly owe its origin to anything connected with the proceedings of Monday. Ellison and deceased, we have been credibly informed, were both Teetotalers.

The prisoner left this town in custody at an early hour this (Wednesday) morning for Bodmin.

THOMAS, PRINTER, PENZANCE.

94

TRIAL & SENTENCE
OF THE SOLDIER,
William Nevan,

For the Wilful Murder of Serjeant-major Robinson.

Tried at Bodmin, on Monday, the 28th day of July, 1856.

WILLIAM NEVAN was indicted for the Wilful Murder of Benjamin Robinson, on the 1st of June, 1856. He was also charged with the same offence on the coroner's inquisition. The prisoner, when arraigned, and asked whether guilty or not guilty, replied "Not guilty, it happened by accident." The prisoner is an Irishman.

Mr. Collier stated the case for the prosecution. He had to call the attention of the jury to a very grave and solemn investigation into the circumstances attending the death of a brave officer in Her Majesty's service. The deceased was a serjeant-major of the name of Robinson, who had the charge of a number of pensioners acting as guard of some convicts in a vessel called the '"Runnymede," lying in Plymouth Sound on the 1st of June and about to proceed to Swan River with those-convicts. The prisoner was acting as Corporal under the deceased. It would appear from the evidence there had been a strong feeling, on the part of the prisoner, against Serjeant-major Robinson, who was a smart, active officer, and had found it his duty to remonstrate with the prisoner on several occasions, for not attending to his arms and some trifling deficiencies in duty. These remonstrances produced a strong effect on the mind of the prisoner, who had been heard to say, "if he finds fault with me again, I shall put a bullet in my musket and send it through his body." A day or two before the murder, the prisoner asked Major Russel to allow him to leave the ship, as he could not sail with Robinson. But the prisoner remained on board until Sunday, June 1st. In the afternoon of that day, serjeant-major Robinson had been parading the men, and amongst others had inspected the prisoner. A man named Sullivan was found to be missing. The serjeant-major told the prisoner to go and call Sullivan to him. The prisoner almost immediately after placed his musket on his hip, and fired. The piece was loaded with ball, and the unfortunate serjeant-major was shot in the abdomen, and said, "O my God, I am shot, I am dead." A pensioner, named Kinnard, seized the prisoner, who said "I have done it, I was driven to it."

Several witnesses were then examined for the prosecution, during which the prisoner appeared very anxious.

Mr. Coleridge then addressed the jury on behalf of the prisoner, in an able and eloquent speech of some length: He contended that the gun was discharged by accident and that the prisoner's story was true that it had caught in the hen-coop. Reviewing all the circumstances he confidently asked the jury for a verdict of acquittal.

The learned Judge summed up the evidence, and remarked on some of its features, and with regard to the alleged absence of motive, he said it was well known that many persons were found to take away the lives of others upon motives which to people in general appeared inadequate.

The jury then retired, and were absent about ten minutes, when they returned a verdict of "Guilty".

The Judge then put on the black cap and addressed the prisoner as follows:— William Nevan, you have been found guilty, after a patient trial, in which every thing that possibly could be urged in your defence has been done by the learned counsel who defended you. You have been found guilty of wilful murder, and it is my duty to state that I entirely concur in that verdict. I do not see how any other verdict could be properly returned on the evidence in this case. There has been placed in my hands a statement from a number of persons. I presume in the town of which you are a native. Any use to be made of it, shall be by forwarding it to the Secretary of State, who will take the pleasure of the Queen upon it. I only refer to it to beg you to place no reliance on it, but to take advantage of the short time you have to live, for to prepare for eternity. The sentence of the court is, that you be taken from hence to the prison whence you came, and that you be taken thence to a place of execution, there to be hanged by the neck till your body is dead, and that your body be buried within the precincts, of the prison; and may the Lord have mercy on your soul.

The learned Judge, in passing the latter part of the sentence, was quite overcome by his feelings. When the sentence was concluded, the prisoner exclaimed "The Lord look upon me." He was then removed from the bar.

Within the gloomy cell I lie,
  Waiting my awful doom.
My spirits shrink with fear and dread,
  My soul is fill'd with gloom.
What have I done? ah, dreadful deed!
  His life I took away;
And I must answer for the crime,
  The penalty must pay.
And must I die a felon's death?
  Ah, dreadful thought indeed!
'Tis better die upon the field,
  And for my country bleed.
The laurel ne'er will grace my brow,
  Nor honour's medal wear;
The fatal rope is my sad lot,
  A felon's name I bear.
'Tis hard to die—alas, so soon.
  But I no warning gave;
With all his crimes upon his head,
  I sent him to the grave.
Methinks I hear his piercing cry,
  "My God-I'm shot- I'm dead !
He utter'd, when I fired there;
  It fills me now with dread.
'Twas evil passions sway'd my mind,
  And hatred that I bore.
That led me to commit the crime,
  Which laid him in his gore.
On Sunday morn, when first I rose,
  I thought not of the deed.

But vile temptations through the day,
  To Murder did me lead.
When I the cruel deed had done,
  What horror did I feel,
To see the blood stream from the wound
  Which none on earth could heal.
I then was seiz'd and borne away,
  Within a prison bound,
At length I was in Bodmin tried,
  And soon was guilty found.
The Judge no hope could give to me,
  But that I soon must die,
His good advice I now must take,
  To heaven raise my cry.
Soon I shall hear the prison bell,
  With solemn warning sound,
Telling the moments I shall live,
  Are quickly passing round,
O may the living, warning take,
  By my untimely fate,
And ne'er give way to evil thoughts,
  No person ever hate.
Let no unguarded moment come,
  Be watchful every day;
Had I--- I'd never come to this,
  My life a forfeit pay.
When I'm suspended from the beam,
  My quivering body view,
Resolve to shun your evil ways,
  Begin your life anew.

John O Harris, Printer, &c. Hayle

Wilful Murder

Of an aged Woman by her Husband,

AT ROACH, NEAR St. AUSTLE.

Taken from the "Western Morning News," January 3rd, 1860,

AT daybreak, of Thursday last, the body of an old woman, wife of Joseph Williams, was found lying in her night-clothes outside of their own door, at Roach, quite dead, and with her skull fractured. As soon as the discovery was made known, several of the neighbours carried the body into the house. Upon proceeding upstairs they found the husband in bed. He was asked where his wife Jenny was? He replied that she was in bed beside him, and called her by name. Upon being told that she was down stairs dead, he said that he did not know anything about it. Marks of blood were found upon his shirt, and on the police reaching the spot he was taken into custody, on suspicion of having caused the death of his wife. He made at that time little or no remark, appearing to some extent unconscious of the situation in which he was placed. He is 64 years of age and his wife 65. After being placed in the lock-up, he told an incoherent story about a brave scuffle he had had with a. woman called Betty Hore. He asked what he was there for; on being told that it was for killing his wife, he said he did not do it. It has been noticed for some time past that Williams has been in a low wavering state of mind, and apprehensions of his committing violence must have been entertained, for on the night previous to the tragedy, one of the neighbours made an offer for her husband to stay up with the deceased to bear her company. The latter however declined the kindness, stating that she had no fear. An inquest was held before G. Hambly, esq., coroner. The jury returned a verdict of Wilful Murder against the prisoner, Joseph Williams.

———➤➤➤➤ O ◄◄◄◄———

ATTEND I pray ye Christian people,
  While I a tragic tale relate,
An aged couple, near St. Austle,
  Liv'd many years in marriage state;
But whether in connubial bliss,
  Or hateful strife I cannot say,
The both had pass'd the three score years,
  Allotted here for man to stay.

On Thursday last, how sad to tell,
  The wife was by the neighbours found,
Quite dead ! outside the cottage door,
  With fractur'd skull ! a ghastly wound !
Cloth'd in her night clothes there she lay,
  An awful sight to gaze upon;
They took her up and bore her in;
  The husband, he to bed was gone.

They asked him where Jenny was?
  She's here with me, he gruffly said;
Ah, no ; they told him, she's down stairs,
  Her skull is fractur'd—she is dead !
I know not how it came to pass,
  Somewhat unconscious he replied;
Although his shirt was smear'd with blood !
  The horrid crime he then denied,

What led him to the dreadful crime,
  No mortal tongue can now declare:
But fearful must have been the blow,
  That laid his victim bleeding there;
Poor thing! perhaps driven from her bed,
  Ill-used and beaten badly too, And
flying from her murderer,
  Receiv'd, alas! the fatal blow.

What were her sufferings ere she died,
  Her agony in that dread hour, As ebb'd
away the tide of life,
  Shrinking neath the villain's power;
Ah, none can tell ; but oh, to think
  That man and wife should quarrel so,
To end in death of either one,
  Caus'd by a sad untimely blow.

The aged man in prison lies,
  For wilful murder is confin'd, Waiting
his Trial—sentence too,
  With that dread crime upon his mind;
Then take a warning every one,
  Let love your every action guide;
Had it been so in this sad case,
  The wife would not a victim died.

J. O. Harris, Printer, Hayle.

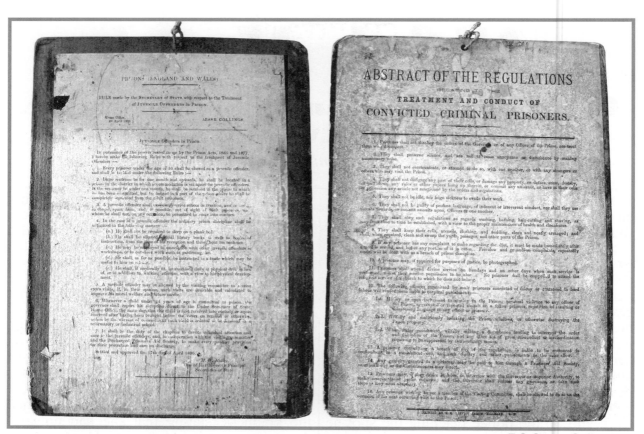

'Rules & Regulations' Board which would have been hung up in the prison.
The Regulations, similar to those on page 59, are dated 1879. On the reverse are the Rules for
the treatment of Juvenile Offenders in Prison (for a transcript see Appendix 5).

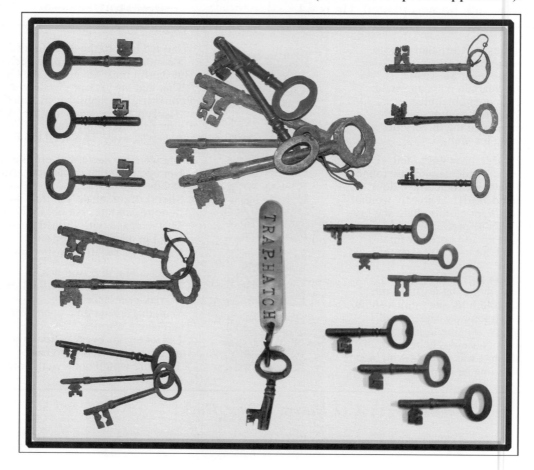

CHAPTER 16

In their Own Words

The Editor's Description (1902)

AN AFTERNOON IN BODMIN PRISON

-- : o : --

Four Hours Inside Without Hard Labour

-- : o : --

A WALK ROUND WITH THE GOVERNOR

-- : o : --

I hasten to make a personal explanation – as they say in the House. My visit to the interior of Cornwall County Gaol was of a purely voluntary character. I had not received the sentence of a felon, neither was I incarcerated as a defaulting debtor. It was simply the result of a journalist's thirst for knowledge – and "copy". It is a generally accepted axiom that a pressman will go anywhere and defy almost any danger so long as he can come through it with a batch of "good stuff" in his hands – or in other words, with a spicy article for his paper. Hence I had not been resident long in the county town when an insatiable desire came upon me to "see the inside of the county gaol". One or two of my more malicious friends had suggested that that need not be very difficult of accomplishment, but I preferred taking a course which would allow of my entering the gaol somewhat at my convenience and leaving it again under like conditions. I therefore, took the most reasonable course and applied to the Prison Commissioners for permission to go through the prison, at the same time stating that I desired to write a descriptive article on my visit. By the next post I received polite intimation from the Commissioners that the Governor had been instructed to grant me admission and to afford me all reasonable facilities for obtaining any information desired.

On one of the hottest afternoons of the year I could have been seen applying for admission at the Prison gates with the necessary sanction in my hands. With the clanging of a big bell the door was opened, but before I had entered, the Rev. C.B. Simpson, who is so popular as the Prison Chaplain and who does so much for the help of prisoners on their discharge, joined me for the purpose of showing me the Prison Library, and of explaining its management. Having shown my permit to the gatekeeper, I was allowed beyond the second gate into the courtyard, and then had free access to the spacious hall upon each side of which are the Prison offices and from which the prison proper extends.

The Library and School

The Chaplain took me at once to his sanctum in which the various library books are shelved. Here it was not difficult to see that an admirable choice of reading matter had been made. From Cassell's Popular Educator on to such works as those of Scott and Thackeray and down to bound volumes of the "Strand", and the "Boys' Own" and the like, there is a fairly wide field of literature. Bodmin Prison not being a very large one the library is not of a very extensive character, but what it contains is good wholesome stuff, tending to the elevation of a prisoner who reads, and therefore to his future good conduct. The choice of the books lies principally with the Chaplain, but his list generally receives the assent of the Visiting Committee before the purchases are made. It was interesting to hear that one of the most popular books among the prisoners is Thackeray's "Newcomes."

The rule of the Prison is that no prisoners serving twenty-eight days or less can have the advantages of the library, but if the sentence extends beyond that, then after the twenty-eight days have been served one book a week can be obtained. When the third and fourth stages of the term have been reached two books a week are allowed. Naturally most of the prisoners who are entitled to the privileges of the library make use of them, and they are assisted in their choice of reading matter by the Chaplain. There is always in each prisoner's cell a Bible, a prayer-book, and a hymn book (A. and M.) and also what may be termed a moral suasion book (generally Bunyan's "Pilgrim's Progress" or the like.)

Somewhat connected with the library and the Chaplain's work is the school. Some, perhaps, will be surprised to learn that there is such a thing as a school in a prison. But it has long been recognised that one of the most potent factors in the diminution of crime is education, and hence the mental improvement of prisoners is not a point overlooked. All the prisoners between the ages of sixteen and forty who have a reasonably long sentence to serve are tested on admission by the Chaplain as to their mental attainments. If their education has already been of such a character as to make it unnecessary to carry them further they receive no attention from the schoolmaster, but where some attempt at advancement is thought advisable the prisoner is put in the hands of the clerk and schoolmaster – warder (Mr. Extence) who gives him two hours' instruction twice a week. At the end of his sentence the prisoner is again tested by the chaplain to see what progress has been made. Sometimes, of course, there are prisoners upon whom it would be absolute waste of time and energy to attempt any instruction and it is then in the power of the Chaplain to leave them alone. The age limit for instruction is fixed at forty because it is thought by the authorities that to attempt to impart further knowledge to a man after that age would be useless. Some of the prisoners occasionally express a desire for this or that educational book, one it may be desiring to increase his geographical knowledge, and another, perhaps with a mathematical turn, desiring a book of arithmetical problems. Whenever possible, the Chaplain complies with the request.

The Governor and Staff

The Governor of the Prison (Mr W.R. Shenton) joined the Chaplain and myself in the library, and after the latter left me to attend to his duties elsewhere I went with the former to his offices and there had a very interesting chat about prison life and prison management, much of which will transpire as I continue my story.

But first let me have a personal word about the Governor. Mr. Shenton has been in the service of the Prison Commissioners for about forty years, and may fairly claim therefore to know the many intricacies of prison life. He has seen much of the seamy side of human nature, and has had perforce to often assume a severe and commanding attitude, but I should judge him after all to be the last man in the world to go beyond what was just and proper in the treatment of any fellow man. He is the son of an army officer, who was in what was known as the 14th Hussars. He was born at sea, and the first eleven years of his life were spent in India but he soon set foot on English soil, and there he has remained to this day. In 1862 he joined the prison staff at Gloucester as an assistant warder. Six years later he removed to Worcester as chief warder, and there remained till 1874 when he went to Lancaster, an old prison with many historic associations. In 1881 he was placed in charge of that prison and remained in that position until six years ago when he came to Bodmin to succeed Mr. Stevens, who had had as his predecessor a Mr. Parr, who was Mr. Shenton's predecessor at Lancaster.

Mr. Shenton speaks with no uncertain voice on the improvement in prison management during his forty years' service. The days of Charles Reade and of Howard have long since passed away, and in their place has come a system which, while seeing justice done is yet merciful and has as its chief purpose the checking of further crime by the ones fallen. I will not at this point give my impressions of what I saw, but suffice it to say that I was very agreeably struck with the system at present in vogue.

The staff at Bodmin Prison is a comparatively small one. It consists of the Governor, the Chaplain, the Medical Officer (Dr. Derry), the Storekeeper (Mr. Masters), the acting chief warder, and twelve warders and assistant warders. This refers, of course, only to the male prison. I will refer to the female prison later. The majority of the staff are engaged during the day, commencing at 6 a.m. At night there is always one warder patrolling the prison and two others sleep on the premises, so that they are within call at any moment. The warder who is patrolling has no keys with him, so that should a prisoner desire anything or the warder desire to enter the cell he cannot do so until he has called one of the sleeping warders who has charge of the keys. This seems a very safe precaution, as one warder by himself might easily be overpowered by a big, strong prisoner. The pay of the warders seems to be a reasonably liberal scale. They start at something about £60, are provided with a house (or extra pay in lieu of same) and uniform. They have to be at least 5ft. 7in. in height and a certain measurement round the chest.

The Stores and the Prisoners' Dress

Whilst sitting chatting with the Governor I could not help being struck with the large number of books in connection with the management of the prison standing on various shelves round the office. But when Mr. Shenton enlightened me as little as to the minuteness of the records to be kept and of the returns to be made to the Commissioners the need of these many books became more apparent. A further chat of five minutes with the storekeeper (Mr. Masters) afforded still more information. The merest detail in connection with the conduct of the prison has to be recorded, and in many instances in duplicate form. The stores are in the sole charge of the storekeeper, who has to account for all out-goings, even down to a single bootlace. When I speak of the stores I not only include the prisoner's wearing apparel, food and utensils; there are also included the raw material which they use in their labour and the goods turned out by them in their labour. In one of the main store rooms on the occasion of my visit there must have been hundreds (perhaps over a thousand) mail bags all ready to go out into use. Coal bags there were also in abundance and great bales of picked oakum.

The governor informed me that the labour done in the Bodmin prison was more remunerative last year that that of any other prison in the country – that is, of course, in proportion to the size of the prison. I believe I am right in saying that over £1,000 worth of goods were turned out from this prison last year as the result of the labour of the prisoners. This is somewhat accounted for by the fact that the prisoners are largely composed of naval men, who have been discharged from the service, and who are true to their designation as "handy men." I expressed a wonder as to what the Government could do with all the mail bags that must be constantly turned out in these establishments. The Governor, by way of reply, remarked that the recent war had made a big demand on prison made goods and consequently there was not such a flush as their otherwise would be. It must be understood in this connection that prisoners make a good deal of canvas stuffs used both in the Army and the Navy. The coal bags, for instance, are used very largely in the coaling of our big naval ships. In the store room set apart for the wearing apparel of the prisoners a very substantial reserve supply was noticeable. There are three grades of dress – the one in most general use is drab in colour, then there is the blue and the brown, which are worn by prisoners who are either in the second division or who are in some other way not herded with the common criminal. The men do not wear knee breeches, as is the custom at convict prisons, but are attired in trousers. Everything has on it the stamp of the broad arrow, and as far as I could see there was not a single thing in use in the prison but what was similarly branded. The shoes the prisoners wear are certainly not exactly dancing slippers, but they are what a good many well-to-do citizens cannot boast as having on their feet – they are all handsewn.

A Surprise

What surprised me most on passing from the prison offices to the prison proper (all under one roof) was to see several of the prisoners all working together outside their cells. They were engaged in what is known as association labour. This, I believe, is of only recent introduction. I had always understood that for hard labour sentences the prisoners had always to do their tasks in their cells, only having the one hour's exercise outside in the morning. But I was mistaken. Here were, perhaps, fifteen or twenty men sitting on stools (one in front of the other) working quietly on the making of mail bags. Talking is, of course, strictly forbidden, but there is the privilege of seeing one another at work and of seeing what is going on around. There is a kind of unspeaking association about it all. It must certainly be less unpleasant than being caged up in the cell all day with absolutely nothing to engage the attention but the work in hand. But this association labour is not participated in until 28 days have passed by. Thus those who only have a month or less to serve are engaged all the time in their cells. The first month of a sentence is always passed in solitude (with the exception of the daily exercise and service) this must naturally be the most trying part of a prisoner's term, for beside the solitude, there is the first fourteen days plank bed, the early horrors of confinement, and the very decided change in diet from what the prisoner has perhaps been accustomed to. Further, what is known as the hard bodily labour, such as picking oakum or making coal bags, comes in the earliest stages of the term.

The men engaged in the association labour on the ground floor were of the habitual criminal class, and the least intellectual in appearance. They were in charge of

100

one warder who, standing at the head, could see all that was going on.

None of the prisoners are shaved close, and it cannot be said that the hair of several was kept back tight. Their beards are kept only as close as scissors will permit. When a prisoner's term is drawing to a close his hair is allowed to grow to the length customary to the man before he started his imprisonment. He does not, therefore, come out of the gaol with the brand on him.

The Cells and a Prisoner's Programme

The cells are all within the same four walls, there being three storeys with corridors are protected by high railings, and even if a prisoner jumped out over the intent to commit suicide he would undoubtedly fail, as wire netting is stretched right across to prevent his falling. There are in all one hundred and six cells, and on an average about eighty or ninety of these are daily in use. The cells are all alike. They are about fifteen feet by seven feet in size, well lighted and beautifully ventilated. They contain the prisoner's eating utensils, all of tin (except the wooden spoon), and shining like a mirror, his plank bed, with mattress rolled up and placed on a shelf, a stool, and the shelf for the Bible and other books he may have in use. In two of the walls, and immediately opposite each other, are two pairs of loop-holes into which the fastenings of the hammocks used to be placed. The hammocks, for sleeping purposes, are now, however, done away with. A gas burner stands low down just inside the massive door. At this period of the year the jet is never required. In the centre of the cell door is a kind of trap door (now not used), through which food and so on need to be passed. Above that is the spy hole for the warders on duty. This hole is covered when not in use by a moveable piece of iron, and in the centre of this is a hole about the size of a pin's head, through which the warder can look into the cell, but the occupant of the cell cannot see that he is being watched. On the outside of the door is placed all the particulars of the occupant of the cell, giving name, date of conviction, length of sentence, what character labour he has to perform and what class diet he is to receive. It need hardly be said that the window of the cell is protected on the outside of the glass by stout iron bars. Immediately inside the door is the handle to a bell which is fixed in the corridor outside. When the handle is pulled, a number printed on a piece of sheet iron springs out from the wall, thereby denoting in which cell the bell has been pulled.

Perhaps it will not be out of place if I give here an outline of the treatment of the prisoner from the time he enters the prison gates. When first received the necessary particulars as to name, age, crime, sentence, etc., are recorded, and in some cases (not, I believe, in those of a minor character) the Bertillon system of taking the impression of the thumb and other verifying marks is put into operation. This completed, the prisoner is passed on to what is known as the reception cells. Here he awaits a visit from the doctor, who certifies as to his ability for physical labour and as to his freedom from any infectious disease. Here he first dons the prison garb and his own clothes go on to the disinfector for treatment. A bath follows (all prisoners, by the way, have a bath once a week) and then he is ready to go on to the cell he will occupy for the remainder of his term in the main part of the building. He is provided with a printed card showing the rules of the prison, by which he is soon able to get an idea of the routine to which he will have to conform. At six the next morning the bell sounds out the order to rise. Half an hour is allowed for dressing and for putting the cell in

order. Then work commences. It may be oakum picking (the work disliked most because of its arduous nature and because of its effect on the finger tips), or it may be coal bag making, or chopping wood, or some other task described as "hard bodily labour." At 7.30 breakfast in served. Following this the hour's exercise may be fitted in, and then there is a twenty-minutes service in the Chapel. By 9.30 the morning's work has commenced in dead earnest and continues till twelve, when there is an hour and a half's respite for dinner. The afternoon's labour continues till 5.45, at which time supper is served. If the prisoner has done his allotted task no further work is required of him after that time, but if he has failed to complete what it is considered he should have done he has to continue his work till 8.30 – the time for retirement. Those who have finished their work by supper time may use the time between then and 8.30 in reading or in meditating on their crime and its consequences. Day after day the same routine obtains, until Sunday comes, when the prisoner rises at seven instead of six, and of course does no work for the day. He attends Divine service in the morning and again in the afternoon, and he also has his hour's exercise. Under certain conditions prisoners who have earned the privilege are allowed to converse with each other while on exercise one day in the week.

Exercise, and the Garden.

The exercise yard is in the open. It consists of two rings. Those who are able-bodied and can walk briskly take the outer ring, and those who are somewhat handicapped take the inner. They are made to move at a good pace and cover about four miles in the hour. They are in charge of two warders who are so situated that they can see if there is any whispering or any other means of communication adopted. In cold or damp weather the men are provided with thick, warm capes, which they take from a rack as they go from the cells to the yard. In very wet weather the exercise is taken in doors.

Some of the prisoners get their daily exercise in the garden. This stands at the higher side of the prison buildings and commands a good view of the whole. Those known as the "star men" generally get the privilege of working the garden. They are men who have never been convicted before and whose previous reputation was good and whose antecedents had irreproachable characters. These men, though they may have long sentences and may be sentenced to hard labour the same as any common felon, are not placed in association with the habitual criminal – a very wise discrimination being shown. The garden is, of course, a very valuable asset to the prison. A large proportion of the vegetables used in the prison are grown on the prison grounds. Most of the space is devoted to potatoes, as this is the vegetable most largely in use. Along the edges of the beds, however, the prisoners are encouraged to grow flowers, and I noticed a beautiful lot of sweet Williams growing in this way as I walked around. Even roses are under the care of some of the prisoners, and as beautiful a lot as could be seen in any gentleman's garden were in full bloom in one of the yards on the day I visited the prison. They numbered one less after I had gone from the prison, but that, as Rudyard Kipling would say, is another story. I will only add that it was taken from the tree and placed in my coat in full view of the Governor. It wouldn't do for people to have the idea that I had committed a felony in a prison!

The Cook-House and Diet.

The cook-house was one of the most interesting parts of the building which I visited (and I believe there was not a part I was not most courteously shown). The room is splendidly lighted from a skylight in the roof, and it has ample space, was beautifully cool even on the very hot day I was there, and so clean that a spot of dirt could not be detected anywhere. It was shortly before supper time when I was there, and three prisoners ("star men") in charge of a warder were busy preparing their comrades' last meal for the day. In one of the big boilers porridge was being prepared and ladled out into the tin cans in a spoon which would certainly be a trifle superfluous for a small family, but which is doubtless essential in an establishment like the Bodmin Prison. Another boiler contained gruel, the difference between this and porridge being simply one of the amount of meal put into the mixture. Gruel is thinner than porridge. In the third boiler there was an inviting lot of cocoa standing, all ready to be served up. It is made from identically the same cocoa as is used in the Navy, and no purer cocoa can be found anywhere. I drank about half a cup of it, and as a bit of a connoisseur in cocoas, I readily admit that the drink was most palatable. On the table by the side stood a sample of the dinner which had been served that day. It consisted of haricot beans, potatoes and a slice of fat bacon. It was not quite the kind of dinner one would expect in a Parisian restaurant, but there was certainly plenty of it, and possibly it is far more easy of digestion that a good deal of the stuff we who enjoy our liberty trouble our stomachs with. I next sample the bread. It is all of the whole meal order, brown in colour, but yet wholesome and palatable. I have eaten much white bread that I liked less. Each prisoner gets a thick chunk of it in addition to the other courses of his meal. The character of the diet varies according the term of the prisoner and according to medical instructions. Whatever food the doctor says a prisoner must have that food is given to him. The plainest fare always comes at the beginning of the sentence and it slightly improves as the term proceeds. Cooked meat is generally given for Thursday's dinner, and Australian preserved meat on the Sunday. Breakfast and supper generally consist of so much bread and either gruel, porridge, or cocoa. Plain though the fare is, it has the redeeming quality of abundance. Seeing the big allowances being made out on the day of my visit I could hardly understand how any prisoner could complain of being hungry. The gruel was being served in a good sized tin, and into the top of that another tin was made to fit in which the bread was placed. A dozen or so of these allowances were being placed on a wooden tray ready to be carried to the various cells.

With regard to the prisoner's diet and as to his fitness for certain degrees of labour the medical officer is the guiding power. If a man complains that he cannot eat this or that food he is seen by the doctor, and future treatment is guided by the officer's decision. Every consideration, too, is shown prisoners in the case of sickness. In the ordinary course of things the doctor visits the prison twice daily, and it is only for a man to say he is unwell and Dr Derry is called at once. But woe be to the man if he is malingering. Neither the Governor nor any of the warders take it upon themselves to decide this point. It is not for them to say whether a man is shamming or whether he is in earnest. Be it any hour of the day or night the doctor is sent for if a prisoner makes an urgent request. And it is interesting in this connection to remark that only one prisoner has died during Mr Shenton's governorship. The prison hospital is provided with all necessary appliances, but on the occasion of my visit there were no patients.

With respect to communication with the outside world, no prisoner is allowed to receive or send any letter until after two months of his sentence have expired. He is then entitled (if he has not forfeited the privilege through breach of discipline) to send one letter and receive one letter per month. He is also entitled to one visit from a friend during the same time. But should his friends live at a considerable distance or be otherwise prevented from paying the visit, the prisoner may send and receive one extra letter in lieu thereof. All these communications are, of course, read by the Governor, before they leave the prison or get into the hands of the prisoner.

The Chapel

The prison chapel is an interesting building. It is divided into four sections. On one side there is the space for the women, coming next there is a space for second-division men, "star" men and prisoners of that class, then comes the place for the habitual criminal, and on the other side is the portion allotted to the naval prisoners, who come from the prison in which they are located (and which is completely separate in management from the civil prison) to worship with the other prisoners. Each portion is partitioned off to such a height that no section can see the other. The arrangement of the building, however, is about to undergo structural alteration, for at present only half of the worshippers are able to see the altar. This is to be obviated by the erection of a gallery at the back which will be occupied by the naval men. The Chaplain and Governor have their places high up in a gallery at the front where they can see all and be seen by all. The singing is led by a large harmonium – a new instrument recently installed in the place of one out of date and, perhaps, out of tune. The organist is Mr Banfield Whale. The singing is generally very hearty and harmonious, accounted for in some measure by the number of ex-naval men in the congregation. Those prisoners professing some other religious persuasion than the Church of England are not bound to attend the services in the Chapel, but as a rule they all like to be present. The service is one of the few green spots in a barren desert and none of them care to miss the chance of a nibble. Within the past few months the Rev. W.T. Gill has been appointed by the Commissioners as Chaplain to prisoners owning association with Wesleyan Methodism and he visits the prison periodically. The Roman Catholic priest also pays periodical visits.

Other Details

I went into what was once the treadmill room, the glory of which has for some time departed. In other words the old wheel has been sold, the Governor "having no further use for it." Public opinion had cried out against the treadmill and as public opinion paid the piper public opinion had its way. For this no one thanks public opinion more than the unhappy prisoner. The maximum amount of money that a prisoner can earn during his term is 10s., but by good conduct he can secure a reduction of his sentence. Sentences of six months or under are "strictly nett" but when they get beyond that a reduction of one quarter can be earned on the remaining period beyond the first six months. Thus a prisoner with a twelve months' term could get a quarter reduction on his last six months. When his term has expired he is released about 7.30 a.m., in time to catch the first train out of town. The authorities pay his fare to the place from whence he came, or if the application is considered a reasonable one to any other place he may desire. He is told to go to the station and a warder in plain clothes meets him there, sees him in the train and gives him his ticket.

There are carpenters' and engineers' shops attached to the prison, and in these some of the prisoners whose previous training may have fitted them for it are engaged. Some really first-class work is done by the men, and some of the mail bags which I was privileged to closely examine showed most careful and precise stitching.

The execution yard is fortunately very seldom called into use. Within the past twenty years there has been but one execution, and that was of an Italian sailor for murder committed on the high seas. This is in striking contrast to the nine cases of the death sentence during Mr. Shenton's term at Lancaster. And this reminds me that the hoisting of the black flag will be seen no more. By order of the authorities (as already announced in the Press) notices affixed outside the prison are to be substituted for the older form of acquainting the public that a death sentence has been carried out.

There is a very complete and efficient system at the prison for dealing with an outbreak of fire. The alarm is given by a bell, and the warders at once rush to where the appliances are kept in the hall and can get them in working order in the course of three or four minutes. Hydrants are placed at convenient parts of the prison and the force of water is sufficient to deal with any outbreak at the most remote corner.

Debtors and men who have refused to pay for the maintenance of their wives or children receive somewhat more considerate treatment in prison than the ordinary felon. But they all have to do some work. They are, however, allowed fuller use of the library and certain other privileges. Men on trial are not compelled to work nor are they bound to put on the prison garb. Most of them, however, prefer to have something to occupy their time, and after they have earned between three and four shillings in the week what they make beyond that amount can be devoted to their own use. They can utilise it in their defence, or have meals and newspapers from the outside; but in some cases the prisoners prefer that it should be sent to their wives and families to help maintain them during the bread-winners' compulsory incarceration.

The female prison, which comes under the supervision of the Governor, is in charge of a warder-acting-matron (Miss Curnick) and one assistant. Entrance to it must be effected through the main prison yard, and the cells, thirteen in number, are simply an extension from the main building, with a dividing wall. On the occasion of my visit there were nine cells being occupied. It is very seldom that the sentences on the women extend beyond six months, and on one occasion during Miss Curnick's three years at the prison there were no females for her care. Their hard labour consists in washing, knitting, mending and so on. They do all the washing of the prison, except in the case of the very heavy articles, when male prisoners are called in to assistance. The hours and diet of the female prisoners partake pretty much of the character of that obtaining in the male section. Both the matron and her assistant sleep in the prison, and though they do not keep watch at night there is no fear of their not hearing any alarm should it be given, or any call should it be made.

Impressions

And now by way of conclusion let me give as briefly as possible my impressions of what I saw and of what I was told. One thing was very forcibly borne home upon me, and that was that hard labour prisons are not by any means such terrible institutions as some of us have generally imagined. I don't for one moment mean to suggest that life inside is pleasant; it certainly cannot be; but it is not associated with that torture, both of body and mind, which is the generally accepted idea. Discipline, and very rigid discipline there is, some confinement there is, monotonous work there is, the plainest of food there is, but none of this is torture. In fact, I can quite understand a certain type of man after he has been in prison for some considerable time leaving his new home with certain regrets.

Though I visited the Bodmin prison the hottest day so far this year the building (go in any part you like) was beautifully cool. The ventilation must be well-nigh perfect. Each cell, too, has its ventilators, so that whether engaged in the corridors or in their own cells the prisoners cannot complain of a stuffy atmosphere. In winter the building is heated by hot air. There is an abundance of light, too, go where you will. The roof of the main building is centred with glass, and in each cell the window is sufficiently large to admit plenty of light; in this respect the cells are much better off than the storekeeper's apartments. Of course, everything is perfectly clean; floors, cells, utensils, garden, cookhouse: they are perfect in this respect.

The treatment which a prisoner will receive during his incarceration depends very much upon himself. If he settles down to his work and to the routine of the establishment with a set determination to make his term as pleasant as he can for himself, in the circumstances, he will find there will be many little ways in which he can lighten his punishment. But if, on the other hand, he sets himself up in defiance, endeavours to do as little as possible and to give the warders as much trouble as he can, he will find that he is making his time doubly hard. Because if prison laws are not obeyed, the breaking of them carries with it its punishment. But even in prison-punishment he will get absolute justice. All cases of insubordination, shirking of work and the like, come before the Governor, and he has considerable discretionary power. In the case of extreme punishment, the Visiting Committee as well as the Governor consider the matter, and when flogging is decided on the decision goes before the Prison Commissioners for consideration before it is carried out. Flogging in hard labour prisons, however, is extremely rare. It is only allowable in cases of mutiny, escape, and assaults on prison officers.

Prison life must undoubtedly bear most severely in the earliest stages of the term, for it is then that the great change from freedom to confinement, from perhaps rich food to plain, and it may be from comparative leisure to continuous work is the most keenly felt. One can get used to almost anything, and I can readily believe that the second year of a two years' sentence can be borne with comparative indifference. I hope the strain in which I am writing will not induce to crime, simply because the punishment is not so terrible as some have imagined. But I should be untrue to the impression I formed if I said otherwise. It may be argued that I cannot speak with the experience of a prisoner. I cannot; but I was not four hours in Bodmin prison, and afforded every facility for seeing everything, without getting some idea of what prison life is like.

And the effect of prison life upon the prisoner? Well, the best answer to that is to be found in the number of re-convictions and in the number of those who must be described as habitual criminals. Unfortunately there are a very large number in this class, but then I would argue that this is due more to their nature than to the effect of their first term of imprisonment. It is almost impossible to keep some men from crime, and the only way in which it can be done is to confine them within the four walls of a prison. But fortunately, there is another side to all this. There is a type of man who has fallen once, but who is not by nature really vicious or criminal. Here prison acts as a decided corrective. Every incentive is given to the man during his incarceration to look with some hope to his life after he leaves the prison. If he be but poorly educated he is taken in hand by the chaplain and schoolmaster and every effort made to make him more fit to honestly fight life's battles when freedom is once more his. Such books and advice will be given him as will help him to have a clearer sense of what is right and wrong, and he will be in every way encouraged in the thought that because he is once a prisoner he need not of necessity be one again. Handicapped he certainly is (that is inevitable after the first fall) but the prison authorities do their best to minimise that as much as possible. And here the merits of the Discharge Prisoners' Aid Society are readily seen. Deserving men on their release are provided with monetary assistance or clothes, and in many instances situations are found for them. It is not always the assistance is appreciated, but the hon. Secretary (the Rev. C.B. Simpson) ofttimes receives gratifying evidence of the good work the Society has accomplished.

As I took my departure it was gratifying to learn on the testimony of the Governor that the amount of crime in the county of Cornwall is much below the average of the other counties. Not more than about half of those detained in the Bodmin Prison are as a rule Cornishmen. The majority of the remainder are naval and military men who have been discharged from the service in addition to a term of imprisonment.

'Bodmin Guardian' 25ʰ July and 1ˢᵗ August 1902.

The Prisoner's Description (1905)
LIFE IN BODMIN GAOL

A correspondent sends us the following notes as the result of his six months imprisonment, remarking that Bodmin Gaol bears a pretty good name amongst criminals for humane treatment.

After a brief record of his admission a new comer receives a pretty brown loaf weighing ¾lb. and a ¼lb. of potted meat, which strangely enough is described on the official printed dietary as "preserved by hot air." A bath precedes a change of clothes and a medical examination. Then supper is the order, this meal consisting of a pint of gruel and 8oz. of bread, the poor unfortunate being awarded an orange coloured badge, bearing his official number, which he has to wear at all times.

Equipped with clean sheets, a pillow slip, and devotional books, he is introduced to his new place of abode, a tiny apartment, in which he finds done up into a neat roll, blankets and coverlet, there being also in the cell a gallon can of water, a washing bowl, a slop pot, a salt cellar, a wooden spoon, some cleaning rags, and brickdust for shining up the metal vessels, and a very small handbrush for sweeping the floor of the cell. Having taken possession a prisoner may turn in as soon as he pleases. At six o'clock next morning a thing like an intoxicated sheep bell yells a discordant summons to arise, and a few minutes later an officer unlocks the doors to enable the man to put out any waste paper, or make any application, say, for the doctor; or, if on remand, for permission to write to a friend or "my solicitor." Cleaning and tidying up and scrubbing follows. At 7.30 breakfast trots from cell to cell, and about an hour later the bell goes for chapel. Then for the first month the prisoner works alone in his tiny abode until 12 o'clock, when dinner is served, and soon after five what is described as supper is handed round.

Then comes another hour's work, and a period which prisoners may devote to themselves till the bell rings out for bed at eight o'clock.

It is no cursory personal examination, by the way, prisoners have to face. They are inspected while perfectly nude in order that not only height and weight, but tattoo marks, scars, and birth marks may be recorded for future use, if necessary. Men who have been awarded a substantial sentence, are also photographed before they leave the gaol, some twice, and various impressions of their thumb and fingerprints are taken.

WORK AND MONEY.

For the opening few days, a week roughly, the delinquents are kept at oakum picking, concerning which there is always plenty of grumbling at their not having done enough. For the first month the work is usually coal bag making. After a month matters brighten up a bit, and the men are allowed to have a library book, which is changed once a week, while they are usually employed on the lighter work of making canvas mail bags, in company with other prisoners, although they are not allowed to converse. A captive also begins to amass money now in the form of a gratuity for the second four weeks, always provided his industry and conduct have been up to high water mark. In his third month the prisoner gets a "rise" from 1s. to 1s. 6d., the following month to 2s., and the following to 2s. 6d. A man may write and receive a letter after completing two months, and at the end of his third month he may have a visit of twenty minutes' duration from a friend. Then, if his industry and conduct have kept good, he is permitted a visit of thirty minutes' duration every fortnight.

At the end of the fourth month a man becomes eligible for any special work in or about the prison, work for which he may by reason of his occupation or aptitude be specially fitted, such as shoe-making, tailoring, carpentering, white-washing, or painting, each of which employment is a considerable relief from the monotony of mail bag manufacture. For the first fourteen nights all adult male prisoners, not over 60 years of age, have to sleep on the plank bed. On Sundays there are two services in chapel with sermons, Holy Communion being celebrated seven or eight times during the year. If a prisoner is of a different religious persuasion to the Church of England he is not compelled to attend Divine service, but is allowed visits from a minister of his own denomination instead.

All inmates are permitted, if they choose, an hour's walking exercise in company with other prisoners. There are various forms of punishment, such as the docking of gratuities, and reducing the diet to 1lb. of bread and water for three days. At the close of the second month the library book is changed twice a week. Prisoners are supplied with clean underclothing every seven days, and leave to bath once a fortnight.

The opportunities for writing and receiving letters are afforded for the purpose of enabling prisoners to keep up a connection with their respectable friends, and not that they may be informed of public events. All epistles are read by the prison authorities, and must be legibly written without being crossed. Any of an objectionable tendency or containing slang are suppressed. Matters of special importance may be communicated at any time by letter to the Governor, who will inform the prisoner they concern if he deems it expedient. In case of misconduct the privilege of writing and receiving letters may be forfeited for a time, but granted again on subsequent good conduct. Nothing in the way of books, money, food, tobacco, or clothes is allowed to be sent to prisoners. Persons attempting to clandestinely communicate with or introduce any article to or for prisoners are liable to fine or imprisonment, and any man undergoing sentence concerned in such practices runs the risk of severe punishment.

'Bodmin Guardian' 15ᵗʰ September 1905.

The Governor's Report (1901)

As regards the working of the Prison Act 1898, I have received no offenders of the first division, and but four sentenced as "second division". Remission of sentence was granted as a reward for industry in forty cases: the privilege is still much appreciated, and is a great incentive to good character and hard work. The provision of part payment of fines has only been taken advantage of by one prisoner, the majority being too poor to pay. The privilege of associated labour has not been abused, except in a few cases. It still conduces to more efficient work under proper supervision. Conversation at exercise has been allowed; all prisoners have availed themselves of it with two exceptions, who asked to be excused. It can, in my opinion, as now limited be safely conceded without danger to discipline or risk of contamination. The conduct of the officers during the last year has been good, and the discipline well maintained. The conduct of the prisoners has been satisfactory. There have been no offences of a serious nature and no case of corporal punishment. There were no escapes or attempts at escape. Hard labour during the first 28 days was enforced by means of coal-sack making and picking oakum. After that period it consisted of cutting out and making mail-bags, coal sacks, seamen's bags, bolster cases, hammocks, and cases, palliasses, tents; also firewood chopping, gardening, oakum picking, labouring, and the usual employments in the service of the prison. The female prisoners have been employed at washing, knitting, and needlework. The condition of the existing buildings and fences is satisfactory. The following alterations and repairs have been carried out, viz: - The chaplain's room papered and painted; a new washing boiler fixed in the laundry; the cover plates to inspection holes of cells have been perfected: the filters at Fair-wash have been cleaned; a pair of large light doors have been fixed to screen off the execution pit; all the cells, air shafts, etc., have been cleaned and whitewashed. The exterior work of the governor's, chaplain's, and principal warder's quarters and front entrance gate have been painted. The old mortuary has been removed from the van shed: new lead valleys have been laid on main roof over female prison: all the extraction flues from the cells have been cleaned; new concrete floors have been laid down in the scullery, larder, and coalhouse of the principal warder's quarters: a part of the principal warder's quarters has been whitewashed and papered: three new w.c's have been fixed in the male prison: a new washing boiler has been fixed in the chaplain's quarters, and the ceiling of the drawing-room re-plastered: the governor's and chaplain's stables have been whitewashed: the drawing-room in the chaplain's quarters has been re-decorated, and the basement floor cleaned and whitewashed. The arrangements in case of fire have been tested monthly and found to be in proper working order. The supply of water is adequate. The clothing and bedding in store have been sufficient. The supplies by the contractors were equal to the samples, and punctually delivered. The dietaries have been good and wholesome. The garden has been cultivated, with the result that the produce has been very satisfactory, the vegetables being nearly sufficient for the prison use. The flowers grown in various parts of the prison have been much appreciated. The progressive stage system has worked well, and has been carried out in conformity with the rules. The rules relating to juveniles have been strictly carried out. The "star" class prisoners have been separated and kept apart from all other prisoners. The rules laid down for the government of the prison have been complied with, excepting in such cases as have been specially reported to and brought under the notice of, a Commissioner.

The Chaplain's report (1901)

I have the honour to report favourably on the moral condition of the inmates of this prison, especially in the case of the males. Their education is very carefully carried out according to our instructions, with results appended to this report. The Sunday and weekday services have been regularly conducted, sermons being always twice preached, and sometimes three times, during the week. The neighbouring clergy have been most kind, in giving sermons from time to time in the prison chapel; and Captain Davey, of the Church Army, held a very successful eight days' mission. The demeanour of the prisoners in chapel and during the chaplain's cell visits is distinctly good, and their attention during pulpit instruction has been most marked. Particularly was this the case during a most instructive lecture on "Moral courage" given by Colonel Everitt, of the White Cross League. I have visited all on reception and discharge, those sick or under punishment daily; and generally manage to go the round of the whole prison once a fortnight. Reference to the Cornish D.P.A.S. report for 1901 will show that a most useful work is being carried on, and that the subscriptions reach a higher figure than in any previous year. I have found the Church Army, the Salvation Army, and the Plymouth agent of the Barnardo Homes always ready and eager to co-operate with me in rescue work of whatever kind. The work of the lady visitor amongst the females is beyond praise, and the governor and prison staff have given loyal and willing assistance to the chaplain in the discharge of his duties.

Reported in 'Bodmin Guardian' 10th October 1902.

John Bull's famous Cornish Inn;
or,
Bodmin Jail, both out and in.

In Bodmin's pretty country town—
　　Though not a place of great renown—
There is a spot remembered well,
　　Where stands Bull's famous branch hotel.

Wheel and oakum, tread and tease,
　　So wearisome and slow;
Crank and jobbing, turn and greaze,
　　And round the ring they go.

Regardless of expense 'twas built,
　　Outside there's neither show nor gilt;
But if you go you'll get a cell,
　　At John Bull's famous branch hotel.

Blue dress for those who are untried
　　And brown for those who have been tried;
But in these togs they look queer coves,
　　Just like pork hams stuck o'er with cloves.

A pris'ner's life's a dreary one,
　　No talk, nor knocking to and fro;
And while at Bull's all sport is done
　　At theatre, market, fair or show.

All things are bleak at that hotel,
　　And not for you my honest swell;
But he who's morally impure—
　　May be turned out a perfect cure.

The doctor tries to keep them whole;
　　The earnest parson strives to sow
The Word into each darkened soul,
　　Though seldom grows a holy glow.

The morning service in the hall
　　Have sacred charms for one and all;
The Sunday rest they pleasant find,
　　With sound-sence books to store the mind.

The breakfasts, suppers, are quite light,
　　With Adam's ale they can't get tight;
The bill of fare's not fare for Bill,
　　Who likes his pipe and loves his gill.

For victuals they've variety—
　　Brown bread of fairest quality,
Porridge, gruel and stirabout;
　　Six months cures corpulence and gout.

They've also bacon, beans and beef—
　　Too good you say, for rogue or thief—
Soup, cocoa, spuds and suet duff;
　　But here's the pinch—there's ne'er enough.

An ounce of bacon once a week,
　　Make many play at hide and seek;
The half-pint soup goes quickly o'er—
　　In vain the dish is licked for more.

Tin washing basin, plate and pan,
　　Tin mug, meat dishes, water can;
Comb, brush and soap, salt-box and spoon,
　　And prayers hung up for morn and noon.

But there are neither knives nor forks,
　　Though plenty screws but not for corks;
Bracelets, but not for Ladies' wrists,
　　Badges, but not for honest breasts.

"System of progressive stages,"
　　Mean a scale of marks and wages;
For first month there is no reward:
　　'The next a bob without the "Hard."

The other two are really bricks,
　　For both combin'd bring three and six;
Though if they one or two stretch did,
　　There's nothing more than half a quid.

The nightly movements on the plank
　　Are something sim'lar to the crank;
It's round and round from night till morn,
　　And glad to rise though sore and worn,

The treadwheel's spirit-breaking task,
　　Like night-mare in a half-closed cask;
Or pickles, sweets, dessert and cake,
　　When jaws and ev'ry tooth does ache.

For breach of rules—handcuffs behind,
　　Belt, birch, eight inches, dark confined;
The penal pound, with Adam's wine,
　　The canvas dress, the cat-o'-nine.

When on triangle getting bashed,
　　Which means tied up and being lashed,
They think—while screws are taking chops—
　　Of glass, and pipe, and fancy shops.

Those dear, familiar sounds we hear—
　　The crow of cock and caw of crow—
Mind of sweet liberty so near
　　To that grim den of silent woe.

The worst's the pack of wolfish screws,
　　Whose looks do cut, whose words do bruise;
Though flesh breaks down, with hard, rough fare:
　　The wounded spirit's worst to bear.

Those who have been to that famed place
　　May know to some there's no disgrace;
For there are some who get a trip
　　To Bull's hotel for giving lip.

Take this advice before we part—
　　Be thou a stranger, friend or foe—
Do what is right, where'er thou art,
　　Lest Cornwall County Jail you know.

PETER S. SINCLAIR.

CHAPTER 17

After the Gaol Closure

In the early twentieth century, although the gaol was still occupied by vagrants and people gaoled for non payment of fines, the number of serious criminals committed was falling rapidly. In 1901, there was only one woman in the female prison and by 1908, there were no female warders employed. Female prisoners were cared for by the wives of the warders.[85] The female part of the gaol was closed on the 31st March, 1911, when the female prisoners were sent to Plymouth.[86]

With the outbreak of the First World War, both criminals and prison staff were encouraged to join the services in the war effort. This further reduced the need for the prison at Bodmin. On the 21st March, 1915, the Secretary of the Prison Commission, wrote to the Admiralty: *'I am desired by the Prison Commissioners to inform you that owing to the low number of persons now being committed to prison they have made arrangements to temporarily close the establishment at Bodmin on the 1st June next. In these circumstances the Commissioners will be glad to know whether the Admiralty would like to have the loan of the building as a naval prison.'* [87]

The Admiralty declined the offer even though Mr Brandreth, the Deputy Governor of the Naval Prison, highlighted some problems with the closure: the capacity would have to be reduced to 90 cells as the other cells would be required for manufacturing purposes, which were being carried out in the civil buildings; the 'Chapel problem', although the naval prisoners entered the chapel gallery by a direct route from the Naval Prison, the Chaplain entered from the Civil prison; and all the heating and lighting was supplied from the civil prison.

The Admiralty was not convinced that they could afford the extra cost of taking over the civil section and the old practice of separating naval prisoners into those who were to remain in Service being segregated from those dismissed the service was breaking down. Prisoners remaining in the service after serving their sentences were being sent to civil prisons in Ipswich and Canterbury, rather than the Naval Prison at Bodmin. The civil prison was closed in June 1916. Prisoners were later sent to Plymouth or Exeter.

The gaol was used for storage of documents of national importance during WWI. The Bodmin Research Project quotes from a letter dated 28th April, 1919, from Anthony Story Maskelyne, Assistant Keeper of Public Records.

'Upon information personally conveyed by the Permanent Head of the Office of Works 7th December 1917 to the Deputy Keeper of the Public Records, of facts in possession of the Government as to German designs upon London, the Master of the Rolls sanctioned the removal of the bulk of the Records to places of safety. That various prisons then vacant were put at the disposal of the Record Office; that Bodmin was selected and a small Committee sat to decide what should be sent there; that the three first out of 24 pantechnicon van loads arrived via LSWR in charge of Mr. Joseph Pratt, 5 Feb 1918, consigned to the care of an Assistant keeper of Public Records sent down to receive them. The last van loads left Bodmin on their return journey 25th Feb 1919. The selection sent consisted both of State Papers and Records. The heating was cut off from the Prisons, the climate was not a suitable one, but it is considered that while traces of mildew are in evidence, the books and rolls have suffered no permanent damage'.

There are reports[88] that claim that great works of Art and the Crown Jewels were stored in Bodmin Prison but 'The Tower of London' website states that the Crown Jewels only left London during the Second World War. One of the claims, that the records included the Domesday Book, could be true, as this document could well have been described as the 'Jewel of the Collection' but no independent evidence of this claim has been found.

By Direction of the Prison Commissioners

PLAN, PARTICULARS AND CONDITIONS OF SALE
of the Important FREEHOLD Property comprising

H.M. PRISON

Two Residences, Eight Dwelling Houses
and Allotment Land

situate at

BODMIN, CORNWALL

which, unless previously disposed of by private treaty, will be

OFFERED FOR SALE BY PUBLIC AUCTION

in 19 Lots

by

Messrs. D. WARD & SON, F.S.I.

at THE ROYAL HOTEL, BODMIN, at 3 p.m. on Thursday, the 7th day of February, 1929, subject to the General Conditions of 1925 issued by the Law Society, as adopted by the Incorporated Law Society of Plymouth, and to the following Special Conditions.

The Naval Prison continued for a time and in 1919,[89] over fifty out of 100 naval men who appear to have given trouble in North Russia were lodged in the gaol. According to the men's version, they had been sixteen hours in action without food, protested in some form and were court-martialled at Murmansk. Some were sentenced for up to five years imprisonment.

The Naval Prison ceased to be used in 1922,[90] in 1927 the whole gaol was formally closed and all the buildings were sold in 1929.

The Prison buildings were sold to Mr T S Lee[91] of Ipswich for 1,000 guineas (£1,050). The Governor's House, the Chaplaincy (£600 each), Naval Villas and the six Warder's houses (£200-300 each) were sold individually and became private residences.

Mr Lee intended to demolish the prison buildings, sell the valuable slate, stone, granite, lead, fixtures and fittings and to make use of the cleared site. The roofs and floors were removed from all buildings, except for the administration building, and all fittings including the slate galleries, cell doors, the pews and all other contents of the buildings were removed and sold. Attempted demolition of building walls was not a success, the lime mortar used in the building had fused with the granite stones and rather than breaking to give clean usable stone blocks, it resulted in

(F.G. Stone Collection)

Bodmin Gaol ca.1930.
The roof of the Debtor's Prison and a section of the main wall have been removed. The slates on the 'Old Quarters' are being taken off but the main blocks still seem to be intact.

useless pieces of rubble. There are reports that explosives were used but again this gave no useful saleable building materials. This failure to make a profit from the stone resulted in the main buildings of the gaol still being present today.

Mr Lee decided to open the buildings to the public and organised 'mock hangings',[92] this was not popular with some locals who considered such exhibitions in bad taste.[93] The chapel was converted into a games room and was used by Bodmin Badminton Club in 1930.[94]

The OLD PRISON, BODMIN

GREAT ATTRACTION!

MOCK EXECUTIONS

will be carried out 4 times Daily, 11 - 30 a.m., 2 p.m., 4 and 6 p.m.

☞ **Come and See how it is Done.**

Just Discovered — TWO DUNGEONS

ADMISSION : ONE SHILLING (Tax Paid).

ALL THE OTHER ATTRACTIONS AS USUAL.

Executions will Start on
WHIT-SATURDAY, JUNE 7th, 1930.

Sir,— May I ask for the favour of a small space in your paper to lodge a strong protest against a poster which is being displayed on our public hoardings advertising "mock executions" at the Old Prison.

That "the last dread penalty of the law" should be burlesqued in this manner is an offence against all the canons of public decency and can only call forth the severest condemnation of all right-thinking persons.

I trust that public opinion will express itself so strongly that this disgraceful and indecent exhibition will be prevented and that those who are responsible for the idea, and who are, presumably, hoping to make financial gain out of it, may be made to feel thoroughly ashamed of themselves.

JOHN B. WILKINSON　　　　**County School, Bodmin.**　　　　**June 2nd, 1930.**

Sir – With reference to the letters in last week's "Guardian" I would like to point out that there is no difference between the mock executions and a real execution with the exceptions that a dummy is used in the former. As the £100 we gave to the Bodmin Hospital, Bodmin Ambulance and Nursing Association was not objected to, why raise a storm? Until those who have written have actually seen it, it is absurd for them to protest against such a thing taking place.

JAMES LEE　　　　**The Prison, Bodmin.**　　　　**June 10th, 1930.**

The next owner, Mr George Smith, used the site for several different types of business, including a haulage company and a scrap yard. The chapel was converted into the '99 Club', which was decorated in a harem theme with paintings by Gordon Quest of Newquay. The Club seems to have been a success during and after WWII. The site was sold in the early 1950s, when Mr Smith's haulage company was bought by Pickfords.

(Mr Christopher Smith Collection)

Smith's Coal Yard late 1930s (Mr George Smith later bought the gaol)
By this time the roofs of the gaol buildings had been removed

The Downbeat Band at the 99 Club c. 1947.
(L to R: F. Angove (snr.), W. Hankey, G. Males, C. Knight & R. Weary)
G. Ellis Collection (D2263)   *Published by kind permission of The Cornish Studies Library.*

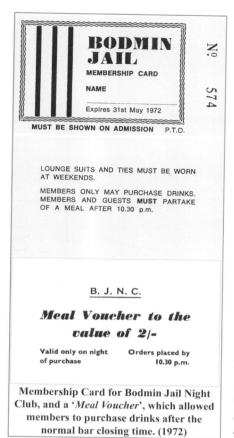

BODMIN JAIL
MEMBERSHIP CARD
NAME
Expires 31st May 1972

Nᵒ 574

MUST BE SHOWN ON ADMISSION   P.T.O.

LOUNGE SUITS AND TIES MUST BE WORN AT WEEKENDS.

MEMBERS ONLY MAY PURCHASE DRINKS. MEMBERS AND GUESTS **MUST** PARTAKE OF A MEAL AFTER 10.30 p.m.

B. J. N. C.

Meal Voucher to the value of 2/-

Valid only on night of purchase

Orders placed by 10.30 p.m.

Membership Card for Bodmin Jail Night Club, and a '*Meal Voucher*', which allowed members to purchase drinks after the normal bar closing time. (1972)

The prison has had a number of owners during the last fifty years including Mr & Mrs Dobell, Mr Kenneth Allen, Mr G Morecombe, Mr Mason, Mr Terry Gilhooly and, the present owners, the Wheten family.

The gaol has been used for many purposes over this time but they may be classified into two groups. Firstly, some of the buildings and the land has been used for workshops and small businesses and secondly, the administration block has been used for entertainment and the tourist industry. The site has been used by other groups, for example, the Fire Brigade (1930s), Bomb Disposal Unit (1940s) and Civil Defence (1960s).

After 1960 the old prison garden contained several workshops and was later developed into a housing estate. The main exercise yard was separated and sold to a local building firm. The Bodmin Jail Night Club occupied the chapel in the 1960s & 70s.

Exhibit: Hoskin Murder

Mr Gilhooly used part of the civil block as a tourist attraction with exhibits based on the stories of some of the major criminals who had been executed in Bodmin Gaol and a bar and restaurant in the main building.

Bodmin Gaol in 2005

Civil Prison   Naval Prison   Administration and Chapel   Governor's House (private)   Chaplaincy (private)

Builder's Yard (private)   Naval Villas (private)   Naval Hospital

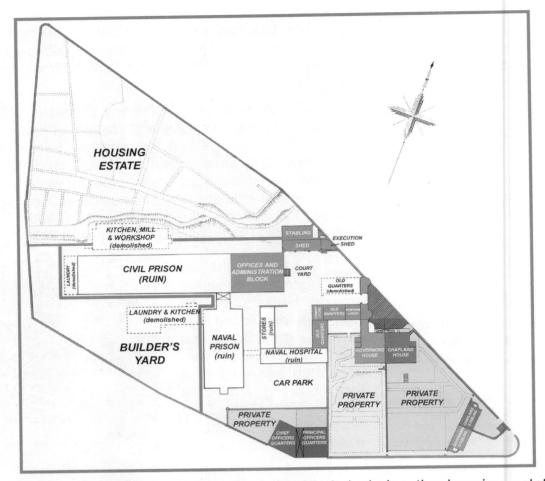

The above plan shows the site in 2005, it includes the housing estate, the builder's yard, the Governor's House, Chaplaincy and Naval Villas, which are all privately owned. The state of the various prison buildings, named as in the 1929 sale plan, is indicated. The only buildings still used are the Offices and Administration section of the main block, part of the old quarters, the main gateway building and the stables/shed. Parts of the 'Naval Hospital & Stores' buildings are used for storage. The lower two levels of the civil block contains prison related exhibits and are open to the public. The ruined naval block is also open for public viewing. The two laundry buildings, kitchens, and half of the old quarters were demolished sometime after 1929.

The Future of the Jail

Bodmin Jail [95] is a unique heritage asset which had been allowed to decay until the Wheten family bought the site in the Summer of 2004. They are ploughing all the revenue from entrance fees and profits from the shop and business back into the Jail with a ten-year plan to revive the site. This will include replacing roofs and renovating internal structures and cells to their original state. It will also incorporate a Museum of Cornish Life, covering the last three centuries.

Their vision is to take it 'Back to the Future' where it will become a thriving, vibrant mirror of the past, a legacy of Cornish history for all to enjoy and a truly memorable day out!

THE 'HAPPY' JAIL

The New Roof

The New Chapel Windows

Appendix 1:

Sir John Call, Bart., J.P., M.P. (1732-1801)

SIR JOHN CALL, **Bart.,** celebrated as a military engineer, was born in 1732. Having gone to India, he was made, before he had reached his twentieth year, chief engineer at Fort St. David; a situation which he held till in 1757 he was made chief engineer at Madras, and soon after of all the Coromandel coast. Having accomplished the reduction of Pondicherry and

Vellore. During a great part of the war with Hyder Ali in 1767-68 Call accompanied the army into the Mysore country, and whilst he was there the Company advanced him to the third seat in the Council, and he was strongly recommended by Lord Clive to succeed to the government of Madras on the first vacancy. But news reached him of the death of his father, and he made up his mind to return to England. He had managed to scrape together a very considerable fortune and he desired to spend the rest of his days in the enjoyment of it. He embarked on February 8th, 1770, after a service of nearly twenty years, and he landed at Plymouth on July 26th.

He bought Whiteford, in the parish of Stoke Climsland, and greatly enlarged the house. In 1771 he was appointed Sheriff of Cornwall, and in March, 1772, he married Philadelphia, third daughter of Wm. Battye, M.D., a somewhat distinguished physician living in Bloomsbury.

Call became a banker, a manufacturer of plate-glass, and a copper-smelter. He designed and saw to the execution of the Bodmin Gaol in 1779. He was elected M.P. for Callington in 1784, and retained his seat till 1801. On July 28th, 1791, he was created a baronet, and granted as his arms, *gules, three trumpets fessewise in pale, or*; as crest, a *demi-lion ramp, holding between the paws a trumpet erect, or.*

By his wife he had six children. In 1785 he purchased the famous house of Field-Marshal Wade, in Old Burlington Street. He became totally blind in 1795, and died of apoplexy at his residence in town on March 1st, 1801.

Call was one of those admirable, self-made men who have been empire-makers in the East, and, better than that, have been makers of the English name as synonymous with all that is powerful and true and just. He well deserved the title accorded to him. He was a man of whom Cornwall may be proud, and it needed no trumpets in his arms and fictions about the origin of his family to make the name honourable.

The authorities for the life of Sir John Call are Playfair's *British Family Antiquity*, 1809; Clement R. Markham's *Memoir on the Indian Surveys,* 1878; H. G. Nicholl's *Forest of Dean*; and *Neota,* by Charlotte Hawkey, 1871, *The Imperial Dictionary of Universal Biography,* 1863 and S.G. Baring-Gould's *Cornish Characters and Strange Events,* 1908 & 1925.
The grant of the baronetcy to Sir John Call, dated 1795, is now in the Museum of the Royal Institution of Cornwall, at Truro.

Appendix 2:

Quarter Sessions sentences for 1812, 1822 & 1832.

Name	Indicted:	Details	Sentence
1812			
Hawken, Samuel	assault	Sally Peake	2m gaol + 5/-
Vean, James	assault	Sally Peake	2m gaol + 5/-
Bartlett, James	taking	6lbs hay	3m gaol
Bray, Gregory	taking	a pound of bacon	3w hard labour
Chapman, John	taking	gallon of wheat	2y hard labour + 2 public whippings.
Chipmas, Richard	taking	12 apples	1w gaol
Cunningham,Henry	taking	tablecloth,stockings,shirt, shoes	3m hard labour
Reed, Thomas	taking	fowling piece & parts	3m hard labour + public whipping
Reed, Thomas	taking	brass pan	3m hard labour + public whipping
Vennard, Thomas	taking	cotton shirt	2m hard labour
Hawke, Elizabeth	taking	2 silver teaspoons	1m hard labour (pleaded guilty)
Jewell, Mary	taking	leather shoes	14d gaol
Morgan, Mary Ann	taking	two foreign coins(dollars)	3m hard labour
1822			
Cock, Ambrose	assault	Jane Doidge	1m gaol +10/- gaol until paid
Cock, George	assault	Betsey Rickard	14d gaol + 5/- gaol until paid
Tanson, John	assault	Elizabeth Larke (aged 9) carnal know.	12m hard labour + whipping
Webber, Wilmot	assault	William Austin	1m gaol
Mallett, James	begging		6w gaol + private whipping
Barnett. John	taking	items of clothing	1m hard labour + public whipping
Boase, Simon	taking	1 lb candles	1m hard labour + private whipping
Cadwell, John	taking	10 gallons of coals	6m hard labour
Cock, Richard	taking	calico bag, a pound of almond comfits	1w gaol. To be whipped
Crews, William	taking	over 120 pieces of wood	3m gaol
Darke, Henry	taking	2 blankets, counterpane	4m hard labour
Davies, Samuel	taking	elm wheel	1m gaol
Fullam, Edward	taking	trousers, dog,hatchet, pair of shoes	6m hard labour
George, Nicholas	taking	check apron	2m hard labour
Gribble, Richard	taking	2x200 lbs copper ore	9m hard labour
Hancock, Richard	taking	10 gallons of coals	6m hard labour
Holman, James	taking	calico bag, a pound of almond comfits	1w gaol. To be whipped
Honey, James	taking	worsted stockings	3m hard labour
Houghton, Joseph	taking	2 coats	1m gaol + private whipping
Jenkin, Enoch	taking	100 turves	14d hard labour
Jenks, John	taking	5 promissory notes(£1), 1 gn.	4m hard labour
Keet, John	taking	bushel of coals	14d hard labour
Lean, James	taking	calico bag, a pound of almond comfits	1w gaol. To be whipped
May, Thomas	taking	over 120 pieces of wood	3m gaol
Moses, Henry	taking	2lbs snuff and a bladder of snuff	3m gaol + private whipping
Prideaux, James	taking	calico bag, a pound of almond comfits	1w gaol. To be whipped
Smeeth, John jun	taking	10 deal planks	3m hard labour
Sowden, Nathan	taking	piece of silver	6m hard labour + private whipping
Stephens, George	taking	2 shawls, handkerchief	4m hard labour
Thomas Dunstan	taking	waistcoat	3m gaol. 'privately whipped'
Vivian, James jun	taking	50lbs copper ore	6m gaol
Warren, Henry jun	taking	calico bag, a pound of almond comfits	1w gaol. To be whipped
Wilson, Thomas	taking	5 promissory notes(£1), 1 gn.	acquitted
Woolcock, William	taking	4 gallons potatoes	1m hard labour
Younis, John	taking	items of clothing	1m hard labour + public whipping
Matthews, Julia	assault	Maria Jordan	14d gaol
Bolitho, Ester	keeping a disorderly house		acquitted

Name	Indicted:	Details	Sentence
Bolitho, Sally	keeping a disorderly house		6m gaol
Farr, Elizabeth	keeping a disorderly house		3m gaol
Haly, Mary	keeping a disorderly house		3m gaol
Downing, Ann	taking	5lbs lard	14d gaol
Huges, Elizabeth	taking	blanket, items of clothing	1w gaol
May, Ann	taking	blanket, items of clothing	1w gaol
Deeble, Bridget	vagrancy	incorrigible rogue	6m gaol
Thomas, Jane	vagrancy		1m solitary confinement

1832

Name	Indicted:	Details	Sentence
Ball, Thomas	assault	Henry Angwin, constable	1m hard labour
Gribble, Thomas	assault	2 constables in execution of their duties	6m hard labour
Hambly, William	assault	intent to ravish Ann Williams	12m hard labour
Holman, Thomas	assault	with intent to ravish	2y hard labour
Hunkin, Joseph	assault	intent to ravish & beating Emma Ford	2y gaol (guilty of assault only)
Lucas, John	assault	Nathan Sturge	1m gaol
Luney, Ezekiel	assault	Henry Angwin, constable	1m hard labour
Morcomb, John	assault	2 constables in execution of their duties	12m hard labour
Rogers, John	assault	2 constables in execution of their duties	6m hard labour
Thomas, Stephen	assault	parish constable	6m hard labour
Whitford Joseph	assault	2 constables in execution of their duties	6m hard labour
Roberts, Charles	false preten.	goods	6m hard labour
Williams, John	false preten.	five shillings	6m hard labour
Bennett, John James	receiving	receiving three £5 notes	6m hard labour
Waters, William	receiving	see Treweek, John	transported seven years
Allen, George	stealing	20lbs rope	1m hard labour
Allen, James	stealing	two barn door fowls	custody until end of sessions
Allen, Joseph	stealing	two barn door fowls	1m hard labour
Andrewartha, John	stealing	100lbs copper ore	9m hard labour
Austin, James	stealing	3 pecks barley & bag	6m hard labour
Baker, Thomas	stealing	two geese	1m hard labour
Bias, Joseph	stealing	a sheet	6w hard labour
Bowles, William	stealing	2 sacks & silver meat spoon	6m hard labour
Bray, Alexander	stealing	100lbs copper ore	9m hard labour
Bray, William	stealing	4 shirts, cravat & handkerchief	4m hard labour
Burdon, Richard	stealing	two geese	1m hard labour
Burnard, Robert	stealing	two gallons apples	14d hard labour (pleaded guilty)
Candy, John	stealing	20lbs copper & 10lbs copper	2m hard labour
Clift, Joseph	stealing	4 barn-door fowls	14d hard labour + whipping
Cock, John	stealing	5lbs. Gingerbread	1m hard labour
Cole, Nicholas	stealing	£5 note	4m hard labour
Coom, Richard	stealing	2x 60lbs tin ore and 60lbs black tin	3m hard labour
Cuming, Henry	stealing	five ganders & two geese	9m hard labour
Dingle, John	stealing	watch, watch chain & key	acquitted
Donovan, Michael	stealing	2 sacks & silver meat spoon	6m hard labour
Dymond, Thomas	stealing	8 gallons barley	1m hard labour
Elliott, James	stealing	10 pairs leather shoes	3m hard labour
Elliott, Joseph	stealing	two hazel roots	1w hard labour (pleaded guilty)
Endean, Richard	stealing	a counterpane	3m hard labour
Fish, John	stealing	glass rummer & teaspoon	1w hard labour
Friggins, John	stealing	horde collar & harness	3m hard labour
Giles, Henry	stealing	4 brass bearings & 80lbs brass	12m hard labour
Halse, John	stealing	five ganders & two geese	9m hard labour
Hamilton, Henry	stealing	five ganders & two geese	9m hard labour
Henning, James	stealing	2 guns, powder horn, 2 barrels & a stock	6m hard labour
Hodge, William	stealing	faggot of wood	1w hard labour
Inch, John	stealing	3 furze faggots & oak pole	1m hard labour
Jacobs, John	stealing	2x 60lbs tin ore and 60lbs black tin	3m hard labour
Jory. Ralph jun	stealing	30 qrt Madeira wine, 2 qrt. Ale, 30 bottles	12m hard labour

Name	Indicted:	Details	Sentence
Lawrence, John	stealing	wood faggots & 50 oak poles	3m hard labour
Lee, Thomas	stealing	pair of leather shoes	3w hard labour (pleaded guilty)
Lewis, Andrew	stealing	silk shawl & handkerchief	3m hard labour
Llewellyn, James	stealing	9 bottles & 9 qts. porter	1m hard labour
Lobb, John	stealing	40lbs flour, sack, loaf barley bread	12m hard labour
Martin, Josiah	stealing	20 gallons potatoes	1d gaol
Menhenniott, Richard	stealing	2 sacks wheat, 2 sacks & 24 gal.wheat	12m hard labour
Nicholas, William	stealing	tin box, medal 2 keys & a thimble	1m hard labour + private whipping
Old, John	stealing	a watch	12m hard labour
Pascoe, Robert	stealing	a gun lock	14d hard labour
Pearce, John	stealing	5 sheaves & quantities of wheat and straw	3m hard labour
Pearce, Stephen	stealing	sledge hammer,2 shovels, 2 water barrels	12m hard labour
Perriman, Martin	stealing	shirt	3m hard labour
Prinn, William	stealing	4 brass bearings & 80lbs brass	12m hard labour
Rowling, Thomas	stealing	mutton, bacon,pigs fat,barley meal, etc.	6m hard labour
Rule, John	stealing	cock, hen & 2 barn-door fowls	2m hard labour
Sarah, Richard	stealing	20 gallons potatoes	3m hard labour
Sarah, Richard	stealing	pair of breeches	3m hard labour following previous
Scawn, John	stealing	a gander	1m hard labour
Smith, Thomas	stealing	pick & mattock	1m hard labour
Sowden, Peter	stealing	two geese	6m hard labour
Stanbury, Benjamin	stealing	2 mattocks, pick,lock & vat cage	3m hard labour
Stephens, Jacob	stealing	quantities of oats	1w gaol
Stephens, Richard	stealing	2 candlestick (iron & brass), snuffers	2m hard labour
Stoddart, William	stealing	bed sheets & bed curtains	12m hard labour (pleaded guilty)
Strange, James	stealing	a sheet	6w hard labour
Strongman, Henry	stealing	3 halfcrowns	1m hard labour + 2 private
Teague, William	stealing	two barn door fowls	1m hard labour
Treweek, John	stealing	2 sacks wheat, 2 sacks & 24 gal.wheat	12m hard labour
Vivian, Joseph	stealing	watch, watch chain & key	6m hard labour + private whipping
Watts, Hugh Bawden	stealing	brown silk umbrella	14d hard labour (pleaded guilty)
White, John	stealing	shirt, waistcoat,trousers, jar, beer & cider	4m hard labour
White, John Guiham	stealing	two waistcoats	3m hard labour
Williams, Joseph	stealing	two barn door fowls	1m hard labour
Williams, Thomas	stealing	a duck	1w hard labour
Willoughby, Oliver	stealing	two barn door fowls	1m hard labour
Wills, Thomas	stealing	4 barn-door fowls	14d hard labour + whipping
Wilson, James	stealing	10 pairs leather shoes	acquitted
Worth, Frederick	stealing	a wheel	1m hard labour
Hugh, Duance	assault	Richard labour Lobb, constable	6m hard labour
Lucas, Mary Williams	assault	Nathan Sturge	acquitted
Brown, Charlotte	false preten.	goods	12m hard labour
Bennett, Margaret	stealing	three £5 notes	6m hard labour
Burden, Ann	stealing	3lbs mutton	6w hard labour
Chappel, Martha	stealing	blanket	1m gaol
Collins, Mary Ann	stealing	£1.13s.	6m hard labour
Ellis, Jane	stealing	a turf	14d hard labour
Hancock, Elizabeth	stealing	several coins	14d hard labour
Harris, Mary	stealing	8ozs. Worsted	3m hard labour
Key, Elizabeth	stealing	3yds lace	14d hard labour
Lampshire, Betsey	stealing	haberdashery, soap, soda, tea & snuff	6w hard labour
Rowling, Elizabeth	stealing	mutton, bacon,pigs fat,barley meal, etc.	6m hard labour
Selkirk, Elizabeth	stealing	linen sheet, feather bed,10lbs feathers	14d hard labour
Stacey, Ann	stealing	piece of printed cotton	6m gaol (pleaded guilty)
Tregea, Sophia	stealing	pair of leather shoes & 2 pattens	1m in gaol
Triggs, Elizabeth	stealing	poker, tongs & fire shovel	2m hard labour
Watts, Jane	stealing	100yds ribbon	12m hard labour (pleaded guilty)
Wills, Jane	stealing	20lbs bacon	6m hard labour

Appendix 3:
List of Staff Employed in Bodmin Gaol

Name	Title	From	To	Born	Salary	Recorded in:
Alford, Beatrice A	Assist. Warder			1876		C1901
Anguin, William	Clerk					K1873
Angwin, William	Engineer	pre 1861	post 1871	1822		C1861, C1871
Arnold, James	Warder	pre 1871	post 1881	1826		C1871, C1881
Austin, Thomas	Chaplain	post 1914	1922			K1914
Bacon, Charles J	Warder			1832		C1891
Barker, Joseph	Clerk	pre 1883	post 1891	1849		K1883, C1891
Beard, John	Turnkey	1779	1786			QS1779
Bennett, William J	Assist. Warder					C1901
Blight, Henry	Assist. Warder			1872		C1901
Boor, Leonard Jarvis	Chaplain	1823	1835		£150 (1823)	QS1823, QS1835
Bounds, Eliza	Assist. Warder			1837		C1881
Bramble, John Thomas	Warder			1810		C1851
Brandreth, Comm. Thomas	Governor Naval	1910	1922			K1914
Browett, Henry Leonard	Governor Civil	pre 1906	1916			K1906, K1914
Cartwright, M B	Governor Naval	1890	1890/1			BG 7/1/1922, p4
Chapman, Samuel E	Clerk/School.					K1914
Chapple, Frederick	Governor Civil	1827				QS1827(Oct.)
Chapple, James	Governor Civil	1779	1827			QS1827
Collins, Thomas	Warder (Hosp.)	pre 1871	post 1881	1824		C1871, C1881
Colvill, Hugh George	Governor Civil	ca.1860	post1878	1822		C1861, PO1873
Corney, Philip	Messenger	1786	1835	1835	£15 (1786)	QS1786, QS1835
Curnick, Lucy	Matron			1852		C1901, K1902
Davey, Thomas	Warder / Miller	pre 1861	post 1871	1830		C1861, C1871
Derry, Bartholomew Gidley	Medical Officer	pre 1889	post 1914			K1889, K1914
Doidge, Richard	Officer	pre1891	post1901	1860		C1891, C1901
Dungey, Ann	Matron	1840	post 1871	1808	£30 (1846)	C1841, C1871
Dungey, Edna Ann	Assist. Matron			1836		C1861
Dungey, Mary	Matron	pre 1871	post 1881	1841		C1871, C1881
Dungey, Mary Ann	Matron	1831	1840			C1831, C1841
Dungey, Thomas	Turnkey	1790			£20 (1790)	QS1790
Dungey, Thomas	Prin. Turnkey	1819	post 1851	1791	£55 (1843)	QS1828, C1851
Edmunds, Joseph	Chief Warder (N)	pre 1891	post 1914	1859		K1897, K1914
Elston, William H	Prin. Warder (N)					K1914
Everest, John Bentham	Governor Civil	1828	1860	1782	£400 (1843)	QS1828, C1851
Everest, William Frederick	Chaplain	pre 1861	post 1883	1818		C1861, K1883
Every, Peter	Third Turnkey	1828			£30 (1828)	QS1828
Extence, Edwin Albert	Clerk/School					K1906
Fayrer, Joseph	Chaplain	1812	1822			QS1812
Gearing, Warren S	Chief Warder (N)	pre 1891	post 1901	1846		C1891, C1901
Goff, Daniel	Chief Warder					K1906

Name	Title	From	To	Born	Salary	Recorded in:
Green, John	Chief Warder					K1914
Hamley , William	Surgeon	pre 1797	1810			QS 1797, QS 1810
Hamley, Joseph	Surgeon	1810	post 1847	1783	£90 (1847)	QS 1810, IR1847
Harris, William	Turnkey	pre 1831	1841-3	1771		C1831, C1841
Harrison, George	Warder	pre 1851	post 1861	1811		C1851, C1861
Hawke, William	Turnkey	1779	1786			QS1779
Heal, James	Porter / Warder			1828		C1871
Hewett, John	Turnkey	1786	1790			QS1786
Hill, Sampson Francis	Watchman	1839	post 1847	1814	£36 (1844)	C1841, IR1847
Hodges, William	Temp warder			1834		C1891
Hill, William	Turnkey.	1827	post 1847	1786		C1831, IR1847
Holman, James	Gate porter	1828		1805	£40 (1844)	C1831, C1871
Holman, Richard	Second Turnkey	1828			£35 (1828)	QS1828
Hurch, William	Clerk/Storekeep.					K1902
Jacobs, William	Principal Warder					K1902
Jago, Thomas jr	Watchman			1806		C1861
James, John	Clerk/Store (N)	pre 1889	post 1891	1850		K1889, C1891
Jane, Charles	Cook / Baker			1849		C1881
Johnstone, Comm. P C	Governor Naval	1891	1910	1843		C1891, K1906
Kemp, Alfred R	Ass. Warder (N)			1852		C1891
Kendall, Francis J H	Chaplain	1835	1845		£200 (1843)	QS1836
Kendall, Nicholas	Chaplain	1845			£200 (1847)	IR1847
Kernick, James	Warder			1855		C1891
Lane, Maj. E W	Governor Civil	pre 1881	1883	1832		C1881
Leach, Edmund	Governor	1779	1780			QS1780
Lethbridge, John	Chaplain		1797			QS1797
Lockyer, Thomas H	Warder (N)	pre 1891	post 1901	1845		C1891, C1901
Luscombe, Samuel Geo.	Clerk/Store. (N)					K1906
Marshall, Adelaide	Matron					K1906
Martin, John	Gate Keeper	1831	post 1861	1795	£40 (1844)	C1841, C1861
Martin, John	Officer			1834		C1871
Mayell, James	Principal Warder			1819		C1871
McAdam, Cuthbert	Chaplain (Cath.)					K1897
McElroy, Alphonsus	Chaplain (Cath.)					K1914
McIlwaine, Captain G S	Governor Naval	1890	1890			BG 7/1/1922, p4
McNeile, Comm. Malcolm	Governor Naval	1887	1890			K1889
Menehini, Felix	Chaplain (Cath.)					K1889
Morgan, Moses	Chaplain	1797	1810		£50 (1802)	QS1802
Morris, Elizabeth	Assist. Warder			1859		C1891
Mules, Mrs			post 1831			QS 1829, C1831
Nichol, James	Warder			1852		C1891
Osborn, William	Turnkey/ Warder	1840	post 1861	1798	£40 (1844)	C1841, C1861
Parr, Mr	Governor	1883				
Pascoe, Joseph	Turnkey			1800		C1841
Peter, Jane	Assist. Matron	1843	post 1871	1812		C1851, C1871

Name	Title	From	To	Born	Salary	Recorded in:
Peter, William	Clerk	1843	post 1851	1815	£40 (1844)	IR1847, C1851
Phillips, Louisa	Warder			1864		C1891
Plummer, George Thomas	Chaplain	1810	1812		£50 (1810)	QS1810, QS1812
Quiller-Couch, Thomas	Surgeon					K1883
Rainford, Robert	Chief Warder			1833		C1881
Ranger, James	Messenger			1835		C1851
Richards, George J	Warder	pre 1891	post 1901	1863		C1891, C1901
Sandford, George H	Warder (N)			1849		C1891
Scobell, Peter Edward	Surgeon	1797	1803			QS 1797, QS 1803
Shaftain, George	Gate Porter			1824		C1881
Shenton, Wm. Repulsa	Governor Civil	pre 1897	post 1901	1842		K1897, C1901
Simmons, Harriet	Assist. Warder			1837		C1881
Simpson, Charles B	Chaplain	pre 1891	post 1901	1849		C1891, C1901
Smith, Aloysius	Chaplain (Cath.)					K1906
Sowden, Henry	Warder	pre 1881	post 1891	1832		C1881, C1891
Sowden, William	Ass. Warder (N)	pre1891	post1901	1848		C1891, C1901
Statham, Samuel P H	Chaplain	post 1901	pre 1914			K1906
Stevens, Mary A	Matron			1850		C1891
Stevens, William	Governor Civil	post 1883	post 1893	1841		K1889, K1893
Titford, Albert J	Warder / Cook	pre1881	post1901	1853		C1891, C1901
Tucker, James	Miller / Turnkey	1836	post 1851	1815	£40 (1847)	C1841, C1851
Walker, Osborne	Schoolmaster	pre 1891	post 1902	1851		C1891, K1902
Wellington, Avis	Assist. Warder			1846		C1881
Wells, Charles	Assist. Warder			1868		C1901
Whetter, Joseph	Debtor's Turnkey	1842	post 1847	1816	£40 (1847)	IR1847
White, Augustine H	Chaplain (Cath.)					K1893
White, Elizabeth	Matron's Assist.			1829		C1861
White, Thomas	TK /Shoemaker	1828	post 1851	1800	£40 (1847)	C1841, C1851
White, Thomas	ReceivingWarder			1829		C1861
White, Wm. Thomas	Prin. Warder (N)	pre 1891	post 1906	1850		C1891, K1906
Worth, Joseph	Engineer			1848		C1881

Key:

C = Census (year)
K = Kelly's Directory of Cornwall or Devon & Cornwall (year)
IR = Inspector of Prisons Report (year)
PO = Post Office Directory (year)
QS = Quarter Sessions (year)
BG = Bodmin Guardian

Appendix 4:

Numbers and Disposal of Prisoners (Year Ending Sept. 1846)

Number of Prisoners.	Male	Female	Total
Prisoners at start of year	20	8	28
Committed for trial during year	143	45	188
Rendered in court for trial during year	55	15	70
Total	**218**	**68**	**286**
How Disposed of.			
Bodmin Prison	105	36	141
Transportation	17	3	20
Sentence deferred	1		1
Whipped, Fined or Sureties	3	1	4
Acquitted at the Bar	36	11	47
No Bills Found	23	7	30
Not Prosecuted	4	1	5
Acquitted as Insane	1		1
Gave Crown Evidence	3		3
Left at end of year	25	9	34
Total	**218**	**68**	**286**

Summary Convictions	Male	Female	Total
Commencement of year	37	11	48
Deserters	1		1
Under the Game Laws	5		5
Under the Revenue Laws	1		1
Under the Bastardy Laws	21		21
Under the Vagrant Act	70	40	110
Under the Trespass Act	14	15	29
Under the Larceny Act	15	7	22
For Assaults	33	8	41
For want of Sureties	12	2	14
Others	63	24	87
Total	**235**	**96**	**331**

Debtors	Male	Female	Total
Commencement of year	6		6
In Execution	19	3	22
In Execution from Courts of Request	4		4
Forfeitures or Contempt	8	1	9
Total	**31**	**4**	**35**

Appendix 5:

PRISONS (ENGLAND AND WALES)

RULE made by the SECRETARY of STATE with respect to the Treatment of JUVENILE OFFENDERS in PRISON.

Home Office,
29 April 1896.

JESSE COLLINGS

JUVENILE Offenders in Prison.

IN pursuance of the powers vested in me by the Prison Acts, 1865 and 1877, I hereby make the following Rules with respect to the treatment of Juvenile Offenders :—

1. Every prisoner under the age of 16 shall be classed as a juvenile offender, and shall be treated under the following Rules :—

2. If the sentence be for one month and upwards, he shall be located in a prison in the district in which accommodation is set apart for juvenile offenders. If the sentence be under one month, he shall be retained in the prison to which he has been committed, but be lodged in a part of the prison where he shall be completely separated from the adult prisoners.

3. A juvenile offender shall exercise, receive school instruction, and be seated in chapel, apart from, and, if possible, out of sight of adult prisoners, with whom he shall not, on any occasion, be permitted to come into contact.

4. In the case of a juvenile offender the ordinary prison discipline shall be mitigated in the following manner :—

(a.) He shall not be required to sleep on a plank bed.

(b.) He shall be allowed special library books as well as books of instruction, from the time of his reception and throughout his sentence.

(c.) He may be employed in association with other juvenile offenders in workshops, or in out-door work such as gardening, &c.

(d.) He shall, as far as possible, be instructed in a trade which may be useful to him on release.

(e.) He shall, if medically fit, be exercised daily at physical drill in lieu of, or in addition to, walking exercise, with a view to his physical development.

5. A juvenile offender may be allowed by the visiting committee to receive extra visits, if, in their opinion, such visits are desirable and calculated to improve his moral welfare and future career.

6. Whenever a child under 14 years of age is committed to prison, the governor shall report his reception direct to the Under Secretary of State, Home Office, the same day that the child is first received into custody or again received after having been brought before the court on remand or otherwise, unless by the warrant of commitment such child is ordered to be detained in a reformatory or industrial school.

7. It shall be the duty of the chaplain to devote individual attention and care to the juvenile offenders, and, in co-operation with the visiting committee and the Discharged Prisoners' Aid Society, to make every possible provision for their protection and care on discharge.

Settled and approved the 17th day of April 1896.

M. W. Ridley,
One of Her Majesty's Principal
Secretaries of State.

158.

References & Notes:

1. 'Imperial Dictionary of Universal Biography' *(Pub. Mackenzie)*, Vol. XI, **1863,** p939.
2. 'The State of Prisons by John Howard' *(Pub. J M Dent & Sons)*, **1929.**
3. John Howard in 'The State of Prisons in England and Wales with Preliminary Observations……..', *(Printed by Wm. Eyres)*, **1777.**
4. Document: CL/1236. *Cornwall Record Office.*
5. Document: QS/1/3/404-422. *Cornwall Record Office.*
6. Document: QS/1/4/56 & 57. *Cornwall Record Office.*
7. 18 George III. cap.17, **1778.** *Bodmin Town Museum.*
8. Engraving **1779**: Drawer 59; Set 2; No. 36. *Sir John Soane's Museum, London.*
9. Ordinance Survey Map by R K Dawson. Published in 'Report from Commissioners: Municipal Corporation Boundaries. Bodmin.' **After 1832.**
10. S.Baring-Gould in 'Cornish Characters and Strange Events', 2nd Series, **1925,** p196.
11. Document: QS/1/12/150-3. *Cornwall Record Office.*
12. 9th Report of the Inspectors of Prisons, III Southern & Western District, **1844,** p48.
13. 12th Report of the Inspectors of Prisons, III Southern & Western District, *Parliamentary Papers,* **1847-48,** [908.] XXXV. 1. British Library.
14. Cyrus Redding in 'An Illustrated Itinerary of the County of Cornwall' *(Pub. How and Parsons)*, **1842.**
15. Document: QS/1/11/614-657. *Cornwall Record Office.*
16. Report of the 'Bodmin Research Project', **1986.** *Bodmin Library.*
17. The Tithe map of 1840 for Bodmin Town & Bodmin Borough has recently been digitised and correlated with the apportionment details by J M & W H Johnson for Bodmin Town Museum.
18. Document: AD 194/1/pages/187. *Cornwall Record Office.*
19. Document: X/106/41. *Cornwall Record Office.*
20. 'Gaol Act of 1823': 4 George IV, cap.64..
21. S J Pocock in 'Behind Bars. A Chronicle of Bodmin Gaol' *(Pub. S J Pocock)*, **1998.**
22. 26th Report of the Inspectors of Prisons, Southern Districts, *Parliamentary Papers,* **1861,** XXIX. 1. *British Library.*
23. 'Particulars for the Sale of H M Prison, Bodmin', D Ward & Sons, Plymouth, **1929.** *Bodmin Town Museum.*
24. P J C Davies. Personal Communication.
25. L E Long in 'An Old Cornish Town', *(Pub. Bodmin Books Limited)*, **1975.**
26. 31st Report of the Inspectors of Prisons, Southern Districts, *Parliamentary Papers,* **1866,** XXXVII. 1. *British Library.*
27. Kelly's Directory of Cornwall, **1889.**
28. Kelly's Directory of Cornwall, **1906**
29. 39th Report of the Inspectors of Prisons, Southern Districts, *Parliamentary Papers,* **1875,** XXXVII. 1. *British Library.*
30. 42nd Report of the Inspectors of Prisons, Southern Districts, *Parliamentary Papers,* **1878,** XLI. 1. *British Library.*
31. Document: QS/HD/354. November 1853. Cornwall Record Office.
32. Ordinance Survey Map, **1881.** *Bodmin Town Museum.*
33. 'Bodmin Research Project, research Material – Maps'. **1986.** *Bodmin Library.*
34-39. Acts of Parliament cited in 'Meet the Prisoner' by John A. F. Watson, *(Pub. Jonathan Cape)*, **1939.** 1779, 19 Geo. III, cap. 74: 1782, 22 Geo. III, cap. 64: 1784, 24 Geo. III, cap. 55: 1791, 31 Geo. III, cap. 46: 1815, 55 Geo. III, cap. 50: 1835, 5 & 6 Guil. IV, cap. 38.
40-44. Acts of Parliament (held in Statute Books by Bodmin Town Museum): 1839, 2 & 3 Vict., cap. 56: 1865, 28 & 29 Vict., cap. 126: 1869, 32 & 33 Vict., cap. 62: 1869, 32 & 33 Vict., cap. 71: 1877, 40 & 41 Vict., cap. 21.
45. Act of Parliament: 1898, 61 & 62 Vict., cap. 41.
46. Document: RP/245. *Cornwall Record Office.*
47. Document: RP/236. *Cornwall Record Office.*
48. Document: D70. *Bodmin Town Museum.*
49. Documents: D119. Calendars dated 1913 -1920. *Bodmin Town Museum.*
50. Census data was collected from the following sources:
    1831: Bodmin Register, **1831.** *Bodmin Library.*
    1841: Cornwall Online Census Project. *(///freepages.genealogy.rootsweb.com)*
    1851: Transcript. *Bodmin Library.*
    1861: Cornwall Online Census Project. *(///freepages.genealogy.rootsweb.com)*
    1871: Microfiche. *Bodmin Library.*
    1881: *www.familysearch.org*

1891:   Cornwall Online Census Project. *(///freepages.genealogy.rootsweb.com)*
1901:   *www.1901censusonline.com*

51. Cornwall Record Office holdings may be searched at *www.a2a.org.uk*
52. Directories may be searched at *www.historicaldirectories.org* (University of Leicester)
53. *Bodmin (Cornish) Guardian*: bound volumes from 1901 to ca.1977 held at Bodmin Town Museum.
54. 'Report printed by order of the Honourable Court of Aldermen of the City of London, 1815' as reported in *'Bodmin Guardian'*, 20th October, **1927.**
55. Document: HO 45/9695/A49760. *The National Archives.*
56. Document: QS/1/4/250-258. *Cornwall Record Office.*
57. James Neild, *'Remarks on Prisons, Lunaticks, &c.',* Gentleman's Magazine, **1804,** p610.
58. Document: QS/1/11/525-528. *Cornwall Record Office.*
59. Tony Philp, *'A Social History of Bodmin Union Workhouse',* (Pub. Bodmin Town Museum), **2005.**
60. Quarter Sessions Records: QS/1/11/668-71 (**1830**); QS/1/12/74 (**1831**); QS/1/12/209-12 (**1832**); QS/1/12/329-32 (**1833**); QS/1/12/434-6 (**1834**). *Cornwall Record Office.*
61. Data from the *Office of National Statistics.*
62. Document: QS/1/10/474-8. *Cornwall Record Office.*
63. Document: QS/1/12/190-6. *Cornwall Record Office.*
64. John A. F. Watson, *'Meet the Prisoner'* (Pub. Jonathan Cape), **1939,** p49.
65. Alan Brunton, *'Bodmin Gaol'* (Pub. Bodmin Gaol), 1995.
66. R. M. Barton, *'Life in Cornwall in the Early Nineteenth Century'* (Pub. Dyllansow Truran), **1997**, p162.
67. Sidney & Beatrice Webb, *'English Prisons under Local Government'* (Pub. Longmans, Green & Co.), **1922**, p102.
68. R. M. Barton, *'Life in Cornwall in the Mid Nineteenth Century'* (Pub. D. Bradford Barton, Ltd.), **1971**, p104.
69. Quarter Sessions Records: QS/1/11/525-8 (**1829**); QS/1/12/75-6 (**1831**); QS/1/12/209-12 (**1832**); QS/1/12/329-32 (**1833**); QS/1/12/434-6 (**1834**). *Cornwall Record Office.*
70. Reference 68, p53.
71. Quarter Sessions Records: QS/1/11/525-8 (**1829**); QS/1/11/668-71 (**1830**); QS/1/12/76 (**1831**); QS/1/12/150-3 (**1832**); QS/1/12/209-12 (**1832**); QS/1/12/329-32 (**1833**); QS/1/12/434-6 (**1834**); QS/1/12/520-3 (**1835**). *Cornwall Record Office.*
72. Reference 68, p45.
73. *'Bodmin Guardian'*, 10th October, **1902.**
74. Document: QS/1/6/1-34 (**1784**). *Cornwall Record Office.*
75. Document: QS/1/6/146/1-158/1 (**1790**). *Cornwall Record Office.*
76. Reference 66, p33.
77. Document: QS/1/11/370-97 (**1828**). *Cornwall Record Office.*
78. Reference 66, p181.
79. Reference 66, p207.
80. Reference 66, p237.
81. Document: HC/CL/JO/10/169/218. *'Naval Prisons Regulations'*, **1892**. *House of Lords Record Office.*
82. Document: HC/CL/JO/10/198/105. *'Naval Prison Regulations, revised to bring into agreement with Local Prisons'* **1900**. *House of Lords Record Office.*
83. *'Bodmin Guardian'*, 7th February, **1929,** p6.
84. R. M. Barton, *'Life in Cornwall in the Late Nineteenth Century'* (Pub. D. Bradford Barton, Ltd.), **1972**, p97.
85. *'Bodmin Guardian'*, 3rd July, **1908,** p5.
86. *'Bodmin Guardian'*, 2nd June, **1911,** p5.
87. Document: ADM 1/8451/64. *The National Archives.*
88. *'Bodmin Guardian'*, 24th January, **1929**.
89. *'Bodmin Guardian'*, 5th December, **1919**.
90. *'Bodmin Guardian'*, 27th January, **1922.**
91. *'Bodmin Guardian'*, 14th February, **1929,** p4.
92. *'Bodmin Guardian'*, 5th June, **1930,** p14.
93. *'Bodmin Guardian'*, 12th June, **1930,** p7.
94. *'Bodmin Guardian'*, 5th November, **1931,** p4.
95. www.bodminjail.org

List of Illustrations

List of Charts and Tables

'Go to Jail'

No. 98.

5 Geo. IV. c. 83, sec. 3.
Commitment of an Idle and
Disorderly Person.

To the Constable of the County of Cornwall, and to the Keeper of His Majesty's Prison at Bodmin, in the County of Cornwall.

DIVISION OF
~~EAST~~ NORTH,
COUNTY OF
CORNWALL
(to wit).

Whereas & *Joel Henry Lucas* of *no fixed residence* in the said County, was this day duly convicted before the undersigned, one of His Majesty's Justices of the Peace in and for the said County of Cornwall, of being an Idle and Disorderly Person within the intent and meaning of the Statute of the Fifth Year of the reign of His late Majesty King George IV., chapter 83; for that he the said *Joel Henry Lucas* on the *20th* day of *November* in the year of our Lord One thousand nine hundred and *seven* at *Pipers Pool* in the Parish of *Trewen* ~~unlawfully did aid abet counsel and procure~~ in the said County, unlawfully ~~did~~ wander abroad ~~[or place him self]~~ in a certain public ~~place [or street,~~ highway, ~~court or passage]~~ there called *Pipers Pool* to beg alms, contrary to the Form of the Statute in such case made and provided, and was by me, the said Justice, adjudged and ordered to be committed for the said offence to His Majesty's Prison at Bodmin aforesaid, there to be kept to *hard labour for the space of* *Ten days.*

This sentence to commence from this date.

L Thompson

These are therefore to command you, the said Constable of the County of Cornwall, to take the said *Joel Henry Lucas* and him safely convey to His Majesty's Prison at Bodmin aforesaid, and there to deliver him to the Keeper thereof, together with this Warrant; and I do hereby command you, the said Keeper, so receive the said *Joel Henry Lucas* into your Custody in His Majesty's Prison, there to imprison him and keep him to *hard labour for the space of* *Ten days.* and for so doing this shall be your sufficient Warrant.

Given under my Hand and Seal this *20th* day of *November* in the Year of our Lord One thousand nine hundred and *seven* at Launceston, in the said County.

L Thompson

Shaw & Sons, Fetter Lane, E.C.
(7356—06)

A Committal Document, dated 1907.
(Found by Ken & Beryl Allen under the floorboards in the mid-1960s, when they owned the Jail.)